2012 Best of The Spit Take

A Compilation of Professional Comedy Criticism

2012 Best of The Spit Take

Edited by Julie Seabaugh
Editorial Assistant – Daniel Berkowitz

All contents Copyright © 2013

Published by Paradisiac Publishing.

Cover art by TJ Young

ISBN:9780985316860

"If you're in a band and you're just starting out, you'll get a fucking article in Rolling Stone, *fer Chrissake. Everyone loves music and bands, but comedy, we don't get no respect, man. No one writes about comedy; no one gives a fuck about it. And I think there's some great comedians out there, you know? I think it's fucking sad we're overlooked. Like, as a musician, you can look up to U2 or someone cool, but as a fucking comedian, my U2 is Don Rickles. It just don't have the same fucking effect on people."* —Mitch Hedberg

Contents

Introduction

For the comedy world, 2012 marked a year of sweeping change. It was a year of emergence, with up-and-coming local scenes in Atlanta, Denver, and Portland proving their worth on a national level as fertile grounds for breeding talent and cultivating festivals. Individually, James Adomian's impressions of public figures, fictional villains, and fellow comedians blew minds from coast to coast; such smoking-hot commodities as Michael Che, Rory Scovel, Emily Heller, Joe Mande, Nate Bargatze, and the trio behind *The Grawlix* (Ben Roy, Andrew Overdahl, and Adam Cayton-Holland) didn't fare too badly over the past 12 months, either.

It was a year of remembrance, as not one but two posthumous Patrice O'Neal releases and the death of Phyllis Diller arrived all too soon following Greg Giraldo's fatal 2010 overdose and a heart attack felling Mike DeStefano in early 2011.

It was a year of revelation; Todd Glass came out of the closet on *WTF with Marc Maron*, Tig Notaro worked through her fear of the life-altering unknown onstage, and memoirs by Sara Benincasa and Moshe Kasher offered harrowing glimpses into a few of the dark neuroses plaguing many more hearts and minds beneath the stand-up spotlight than general audiences would ever realize.

It was a year of revolution, with Louis C.K. disrupting the traditional models of production and distribution with a self-made, minimally promoted, direct-to-fans downloading experience subsequently replicated by Aziz Ansari, Jim Gaffigan, Rob Delaney, and Maria Bamford. The institution of the cable-event special was also redefined, with Jim Norton and Lewis Black eschewing the likes of HBO and Showtime for EPIX, while Bill Burr, Todd Glass, and Moshe Kasher premiered efforts directly via Netflix. (Bonus point for the phoenix rebirth of *Arrested Development*, the fourth season of which premieres this spring on the streaming giant, seven years after the final original episode.) Album-wise, more debuts were self-released digitally (and via iTunes) than ever before.

And speaking of Louis C.K., it was a triumphant year for quality, mold-breaking television programming; *Louie* won two Emmy awards, *Portlandia* kept the hipster hijinks a-rolling, *Comedy Bang! Bang!* legitimized the notion of live-show-turned-radio-show-turned-podcast-turned-TV-show, and both *The Eric Andrè Show* and *Totally Biased with W. Kamau Bell* commandeered well-deserved platforms for their fast-rising titular stars. Though it canned *The Green Room with Paul Provenza*, Showtime did bring *Dave's Old Porn* back for an Attell-erific second season, and Provenza can take solace in the juggernaut success of he and Troy Conrad's improvised stand up free-for-all *The Set List*, which has proven so popular at every major comedy festival in the world that the UK's Sky Atlantic HD channel was quick to order a televised version. And though good things *30 Rock* and *The Office* must end (and the *Community* Powers That Be gave an undignified middle finger to creator Dan Harmon), *Parks and Recreation* has more than capitalized on its original potential, and Adult Swim continues to graciously offer day wages to some of the most out-there talents in the industry. Meanwhile, on the big screen, comparatively limited runs didn't prevent Mike Birbiglia's *Sleepwalk With Me* and Steven Feinartz's portrait of Eddie Pepitone (*The Bitter Buddha*) from emerging as the year's best narrative feature and documentary, respectively.

Elsewhere, antiquated comedy clubs and chains that refuse to evolve are paying the price in empty seats, the popularity and financial viability of web series are exploding, well-timed and liberally retweeted 140-character quips can attract more new fans than a typical live set, "If you're a comedian, it's not mandatory that you have a podcast, but I expect that law will be passed soon" (March 2, 2012, *LA Weekly* interview with Dana Gould), DIY is king, and the once-outlying "alternative" genre of comedy is now the mainstream norm.

Comedy is cool again. Perhaps cooler than it's ever been. Yet in traditional media, coverage of the stand-up world still tends to get lumped in with that of music. Why is it that unlike music, film, literature, theater, architecture, or television, the public perception of comedy remains that of mere good-timey, alcohol-enhanced, interactive sideshow as opposed to legitimate art form? In print and online, there are knowledgeable, unbiased, professional writers debating and deconstructing everything from sports and fashion to food and video games. Where are the great comedy critics?

We'd like to think that we've found a few of them already. The reviewers dissecting the 50 releases within these pages (culled from some 150-plus pieces published between January and November 2012) are at the foreground of an impending phenomenon: intelligent, open, fervent dialogue about comedy. These critics provide context, balance, and insight. They hail from different states across the country, and they additionally contribute to the likes of *Variety, Rolling Stone, The Village Voice,* NBC, MTV, *GQ, Spin, The Onion's A.V. Club, Vice, Playboy, Paste, New York Magazine, Time Out New York, Time Out Chicago, Las Vegas Weekly, The Denver Post, The Boston Globe, The Boston Phoenix, The Orlando Sentinel,* AOL, and countless other titles and outlets. All in all, they know their shit.

Two pieces featured here seem to stand out as particularly indicative of where things are heading. The first is Daniel Berkowitz's review of Amy Schumer's Comedy Central special *Mostly Sex Stuff.* Berkowitz wrote an absolutely glowing assessment that dove deep into society's ever-changing perceptions of feminism and sexuality, invoked half a dozen big comedic names, and contained but one small criticism about Schumer's smaller throwaway lines faltering in comparison to her more original, organic material. It was a tremendous achievement. Unfortunately Schumer seemed to misread the review entirely; the subsequent Twitter conversation between the two in part read:

@DanJBerkowitz I think you may be projecting. I don't run into that type of criticism ever actually.
@amyschumer You had a wonderful special and I gave you a review that reflected that. I believe my lone criticism was legitimate
@DanJBerkowitz I'm not talking about that part doll
@amyschumer Which part are you talking about?
@DanJBerkowitz everything but that part
@amyschumer You don't agree with the positive aspects of the review?
@DanJBerkowitz yikes. Forget it Daniel. Thank you for your time, good luck

The ensuing online debates between fans and industry alike fostered the sort of discussion typically reserved for other A&E areas of interest…and proved that aside from joke theft and who rules versus who sucks, the finer points of the act of comedy creation itself are very much worthy of vocal (or at least caps-locked) argument.

Similarly, Elise Czajkowski's assessment of Robert Kelly's reissued *Robert Kelly Live* at first struck him as not only harsh, but also outright unnecessary. Why would she think it's okay to say negative things about an album that first came out in 2003, he wondered, quickly inviting (challenging?) her to defend herself. As Czajkowski deftly explained when she appeared on Kelly's *You Know What Dude* podcast, the release was being promoted by the Stand Up! Records label, thus was more than fair game. Second, disparate qualities between works of art must be addressed and explained, and comedy is no exception. Context and historical significance apply to every album, not just those from the past; nonstop cheerleading for every single work released has nothing but a negative effect on the integrity of the industry as a whole. And, oh yeah, if you can't so much as string two coherent sentences together, you have no business reviewing anything at all. Czajkowski stole the show and handily won the respect of Kelly, his cohosts and everyone who listened to the episode.

On the one-year anniversary of *The Spit Take's* launch, we are proud of moments like these, and of all the top-notch reviews our contributors have already managed to produce. Just like all the great comedy continuously coming down the pipeline, there will be plenty more ahead.

- Julie Seabaugh, Editor

Chris Gethard
A Bad Idea I'm About to Do
Da Capo Press

By Steve Heisler

Buried in a chapter about his (to put it lightly) not-quite-right grandfather—the man once set his own lawn on fire and did nothing to stop it—Chris Gethard speaks to his mother in an aside: "[Pa] was crazy…but at least he was crazy in a good way." His mother agrees. "It's not so bad," she says. "You just have to figure out how to be crazy in a good way, too."

The elevator pitch for *A Bad Idea I'm About to Do: True Tales of Seriously Poor Judgment and Stunningly Awkward Adventure* is that Gethard, a Queens-based comedian who hosts weekly public-access pageant of sketch and stunt *The Chris Gethard Show*, has found himself in a lot of uncomfortable situations. But that's only scratching the surface of this frantic, hysterical and essential memoir. Gethard doesn't just happen across weird things occurring or seek them out because they'd make for great stories. He's compulsive, diligent and genuine in his love for the offbeat and the strange. When he's given the unexpected opportunity to live out his childhood dream managing a professional wrestler as the nerdy pimp "White Magic," he says "Absolutely." When his favorite teacher asks for a volunteer to accompany him to a local prison's Scared Straight program, Gethard's hand shoots up. When his school offers a class called "Animal Grooming, Husbandry And Exhibition. Section: Goat," Gethard signs up immediately and pre-names his goat "Jeffrey Timmons, World's Foremost Goat."

Gethard has found a way to be crazy in the best possible way: Embrace it, then tell as many people as possible. It helps that Gethard is a fantastic storyteller. *Bad Idea*'s chapters unfold conversationally and contain plenty of nods to how ridiculous the situation might seem to modern-day Gethard—or really anyone reading the book. One chapter recounts the story of his first kiss, which occurred after three weeks away at a debate camp. While there, Gethard stumbled upon another kid in the shower with a full head of pubes and instantly became ashamed of his bald mound. "I was furious at my dick," he writes. "And instead of suffering quietly, I let it know." So he screamed at his penis for three weeks before returning to an eager girlfriend, and because he was so embarrassed he cut his first kiss short, forcing her to lie on a pillow in his lap for the entire duration of *Say Anything*. She dumped him the next day because something was off. "*It was just my boner stabbing you in the temple through a pillow*," he thinks to himself.

It becomes impossible to tell whether Gethard truly remembers his thoughts or if he's ironically winking from the future, but it hardly matters when Gethard himself (and his lack of pubes) is the target of his ire. He freely admits that many of these situations come into being because his emotions don't have a middle setting; running out of cereal elicits the same sadness as attending the funeral of a relative. Thus when a Princeton student sends him a virus via Instant Messenger, his first instinct is to drive from Rutgers and beat that kid up. The title of the book actually comes from his thoughts just before entering the Princeton dorm, demonstrating Gethard's uncanny self-awareness (albeit with lack of restraint).

Bad Idea also serves as a chronicle of how that self-awareness grows. It starts by introducing outside factors: his maniacal-at-times father, the aforementioned grandfather, the tale of neighborhood kid Koozo, whose story was the stuff of urban legend. (When his mom's friend visited Koozo's house, "Koozo answered the door himself. He was wearing a t-shirt, but was otherwise nude. In his hand he was holding a roll of paper towels. It was on fire.") He continues into his college years with stories of losing his virginity and combating a particularly hellacious roommate, all the while beginning to understand that his manic-depressive nature makes him more neurotic and confrontational than others. The final few chapters demonstrate that even as a medicated adult he can become unnerved, like when an awkward afternoon with a girlfriend at Coney Island leads to a ridiculous STD scare. This is the part of the book where the material, like Gethard himself, becomes tamer, but Gethard can electrify even an odd-if-not-routine story about a colonic with the opening line, "Doing diarrhea onto another person's hands is the sort of thing you don't know you want to do until you do it."

Gethard is engaging and endearing, humbling himself at every opportunity with as much humiliating detail as possible. And like *The Chris Gethard Show*, the audience is as much an active part of the story as Gethard himself. There he encourages them to call in with heckles; here he encourages them to embrace their own version of crazy. Life's a lot more fun that way.

January 5, 2012

Kevin Hart
Laugh at My Pain
Comedy Central

By Michael Tedder

In the intro to *Laugh At My Pain*, Kevin Hart and his friends and business associates pray together, then gather around, chanting, "Everybody wants to be famous, but nobody want to put the work in." The chip on his shoulder is totally justified. Before he was scoring high-profile cameos in *Modern Family* and *Fockers* sequels and before he was a popular enough standup to cut a direct distribution deal with AMC theaters for his new special (*Pain* first played exclusively in a limited but lucrative run last fall), he was another catch-as-catch-can comedian and "That Guy" actor.

On the commentary track for an episode of the Judd Apatow cult hit *Undeclared*, star and writer Seth Rogen discussed Hart guest-starring as a religious student. Rogen detailed giving him advice on delivering a line, then burst into the note-perfect Hart imitation he used to get the reading right. Rogen noted, "You can do an impression of him to his face. He doesn't mind." Long before he carved out a name for himself, Hart had a distinctive style and cadence that combined live-wire energy with pensive apprehension. And he was humble. These two attributes have served him well.

Comedy Central's edited-for-TV version of *Pain* is a fine showcase for Hart's physical comedy gifts. One won't soon forget the sight of him using a microphone cord to impersonate his crackhead father's free-range penis, and a set piece utilizing the microphone and a stool to demonstrate the important of a headboard to a man's sexual performance is an impressive display of his inventive mimicry and precise timing. Hart's dumbfounded face is a thing of beauty, his paralyzed mouth open but not slack-jawed, his eyes simultaneously wide open and dazed, his posture frozen. Hart has a skill for shifting from macho swagger to paralyzing terror at a moment's notice, as when a SpongeBob SquarePants children's-birthday entertainer threatens him with violence, or when a woman unexpectedly ups the ante on Hart's dirty talk.

Pain is the culmination of a process Hart began with 2009 special *I'm a Grown Little Man*. After a few years of sometimes relying solely on his off-center, manic energy to score jokes (Hart often brings to mind a nerdier version of clear influence Chris Tucker), Hart the comedy writer is now delivering material worthy of Hart the performer. *Pain* starts with a solemn static shot of Hart looking pensive and "serious" that the performer quickly mocks. He makes his entrance via a ridiculous tube that rises from the ground, and as soon as the smoke and triumphant music fades, he immediately makes fun of the over-the-top bravado in which he just indulged.

Hart has of late zeroed in on a theme that works for him: lampooning and undercutting the alpha-male swagger and you-can-have-it-all materialistic celebration of the modern baller. Stressing the importance of staying "in your financial lane," he tells an embarrassing story about hanging out with NBA player Dwyane Wade in Las Vegas, being too proud to let his friend pick up the tab for a night of bottle service and paying his own way. ("You ever get a bill so high you put it in the light like it's going to change?") The next morning he is horrified when Wade insists they do it all over again. Hart quickly shifts from a cocky rising star with cool friends to an exceedingly dorky family man earnestly explaining how he won't be able to transfer money from his savings account to checking account fast enough to ball again: "It's going to take three business days." The transition from stud to square is all the funnier for its whiplash-inducing speed. And it's worth noting that actually using people like Wade as material for humorous setups is a huge improvement over Hart's annoying habit demonstrated in 2010 special *Seriously Funny* of simply mentioning that he's friends with NBA players, then impersonating them while the camera pans over to Shaquille O'Neal chuckling with approval.

Hart is relentlessly honest on *Pain*, opening up about his divorce, mercilessly making fun of his sexual shortcomings and explaining how he can never quite seem to get away from the painful upbringing he tried to escape through comedy. He's very good at picking just the right detail to give a story impact. That his drug-addicted father stepped on and wouldn't give back the $20 bill that fell out of the birthday card his grandmother sent him is a heartbreaking story. But the face Hart makes when impersonating his father stepping on the money and hoping not to be noticed is a riotously cathartic creation that lampoons his father's aggression while humanizing both of their shame.

The line between joy and shame, triumph and embarrassment is one Hart explores fluidly in his work. Perhaps his greatest achievement is how he turns self-effacement and humility into his own personal brand of swagger.

January 17, 2012

JB Smoove
That's How I Dooz It
Comedy Central

By Steve Heisler

JB Smoove begins his set by dancing out to the center of the stage, cutting the music, dancing in reverse back to the wings and reentering. He ends his set bounding around the stage as King Kong with a Barbie doll wrapped around the microphone, which is swinging between his legs as a floppy makeshift dong. In between there are about six jokes told.

Clearly Smoove isn't a "Joke Guy." He can sell a strange idea on his Stretch Armstrong physicality alone, and thus he's able to extend each bit for as long as possible, pulling every morsel of meat from the comedy bone (so to speak). On his debut stand-up special *That's How I Dooz It*, Smoove demonstrates his uncanny ability to turn the smallest joke into a 10-minute segment that ebbs and flows, building to multiple crescendos that often involve some serious contortions and/or the repetition of words and phrases. It sometimes feels flimsy but mostly reads as a distillation of comedy to its goofy core.

One of Smoove's bits is predicated merely on a hand gesture. After an extended rant about the police, he mentions (after the commercial break) that all cops start arrests the same way: pulling one's wrist back in the most uncomfortable way possible. Smoove is quick to demonstrate, and while marveling at how impractical it is, his mind begins seeking out the positives of what this new wrist position might afford. For example, it makes sprinkling salt and pepper into food a whole lot easier, which he shows the audience a few times. Maybe it could be used for scooping said food onto the plate of your friend. Maybe, in fact, it looks like a swan during a shadow-puppet performance at a child's birthday party, and after that swan commits a terrible crime he can be thrown in jail, which Smoove flaunts by shoving his arm behind the metal bars of an onstage chair.

Smoove grins broadly throughout the bit, too. There's no sense that he's taking himself very seriously; he's perfectly aware of how ridiculous he must look to the audience, and that little bit of self-awareness gives him permission to push things in even wackier directions. It doesn't take long: once again readying his trusty chair as a prop, he talks about women who want him to hoist them up for sex and points out that the more he's aged, the shorter the window in which he's able to maintain that posture. He claims a minute is his maximum, so the audience is treated to a real-time showcase of his prowess, with the poor chair on the receiving end.

Smoove relies heavily on his physicality to sell a joke. After all, the first big laugh of the night comes when he sticks his head inside his white shirt, letting it slowly emerge like a giant black baby coming out of a pristine white vagina. It's all pretty damn charming, but it falls short in its ability to rescue hacky premises. His relationship material comes in the form of "Flip-Flop Face," the look and posture of a woman who spent all day waiting around for her man to return. A few seconds of a hunchbacked Smoove dragging his feet and moaning and the joke becomes clear, but the bit itself drags as Smoove keeps up the impression and lists all the reasons there's no excuse for his woman to not be presentable when he comes home. It's a quick decline from novel premise to opening-act-in-Idaho territory. There are also odd sketch segments that bring the audience back from the commercial breaks, where Smoove sits in a chair and talks to the camera. Stripped of his greatest gift—his fascinating stage presence—these short bits provide little other than a dip in the frantic energy level of the special.

Nothing really lingers, though. Smoove is best known for playing Leon Black, the manic and verbose friend of Larry David on *Curb Your Enthusiasm*. Given *That's How I Dooz It*, Black's exuberance doesn't seem to be a character choice as much as it's an extension of the way Smoove conducts himself in all comedic fashions. When imitating ejaculation using the microphone cord, he twists and contorts his face multiple times to sell the joke beyond the obvious guy-waving-a-cord-near-his-penis level. He jokes about criminals getting into shape on the treadmill and acts out a scene where he's running alongside an innocent bystander whose iPod is snatched by the burglar. He plays both parts—the surprise of the victim as well as the glee of the crook—way over the top and with contrasting physicalities. Smoove effortlessly controls the stage, and even though not every joke works, his uncanny stamina is something to marvel. The guy's a hell of a showman.

January 19, 2012

Bob Saget
The Orleans Showroom
Friday, January 27, 2012

By Josh Bell

There was a time, before his appearance in the wonderfully vulgar comedy documentary *The Aristocrats* in 2005 and his Comedy Central Roast in 2008, when the idea that Bob Saget was actually a remarkably foul-mouthed comedian was shocking to many people, and Saget probably did a little too much overcompensating for his image as the wholesome sitcom dad on *Full House* and avuncular host of *America's Funniest Home Videos.* At this point Saget's family-friendly days are far behind him, and the occasional mainstream hosting gig notwithstanding, he's known primarily for his raunchy comedy side. The kids who grew up watching Saget on TV are now in their 20s and 30s, and eager to hear the former Danny Tanner get nasty.

During his show at the Orleans Hotel and Casino in Las Vegas Saget got plenty nasty, but he did it in such a friendly, open way that the vulgarity was playful and endearing. If he was once ashamed of his corny TV past, Saget's clearly come to terms with it, and he was generous with the *Full House* and *America's Funniest Home Videos* references, making it clear how ridiculous he thought those shows were but also never insulting them or the people who worked on them. He told warm, self-deprecating stories about hanging out with *Full House* co-stars John Stamos and Dave Coulier, emphasizing their strong friendship over the years. Sure, the centerpiece anecdote involved Coulier sticking his penis through a hole in one of Stamos's headshots and then getting Stamos to stick his tongue through the same hole, but it was delivered with the affection of old friends kidding around with each other out of love.

Saget's affection wasn't reserved for his former TV co-stars, either. He repeatedly cited his respect for Don Rickles, but his interaction with the crowd was the opposite of insulting and was seamlessly integrated into the show from beginning to end. Saget picked out a handful of people and did some standard back-and-forths ("Where are you from?" "What hotel are you staying at?"), but then went off on a bunch of odd tangents based on the awkward and/or inebriated responses from the various audience members. It contributed wonderfully to the laid-back, hangout vibe of the show, so much so that people seemed completely comfortable just shouting out input at all times. "Great, now they're all going to talk to me," Saget groaned at one point, but he managed to make every random outburst into part of the show.

Saget wasn't even afraid of being upstaged by the audience, as when he asked one man in the crowd where he was going after the show. "The Smash Club," the guy said enthusiastically, to some applause. Saget, perhaps familiar with Vegas nightlife, asked genuinely, "Is that a real place?" before getting the smackdown from multiple audience members: "It's from *Full House*!" Saget hung his head in shame, and the crowd went nuts. Of course they knew more about *Full House* than he did, and of course they loved it.

That was the way it went all night, like hanging out with your cool uncle who lets you use swear words and tells you stories your parents don't want you to hear. Saget appealed to the grown-up naughty kids who watched *Full House* with plenty of fart and poop jokes (probably too many, really), and used the word "wiener" a lot. He was quite the master of the tossed-off aside ("My mom's a good guy," "My daughters are old now—82, 83."), and even when some of his jokes weren't all that funny, he sold them thanks to the rapport he'd built up with the crowd. He even told some musty old chestnuts that he said were handed down from his dad and got laughs from them via sheer goodwill.

The last portion of the show was devoted to Saget's musical, um, abilities, and there again he was like the goofy uncle who can't stop entertaining. Saget certainly isn't a talented guitar player or singer or even a very effective song parodist, but his half-formed little novelty tunes like "My Dog Licked My Balls" (which inspired an audience sing-along) and the *Full House*-focused "Danny Tanner Is Not Gay" (set to the tune of the Backstreet Boys' "I Want It That Way") were fun in a campfire-song kind of way. Saget kept jovially apologizing for the inappropriateness of the subject matter, which just made it that much funnier. He might have gotten the most mileage of all out of a song even older than his dad's vintage jokes, a folk tune with comical puns about swear words that's commonly performed at Renaissance Faires. "I'm feeling very casual right now," Saget declared in between songs, and clearly so was everyone else.

January 28, 2012

John Mulaney
New in Town
Comedy Central Records

By Michael Tedder

John Mulaney has a joke about crossing the street to avoid teenagers because their put-downs are not only the meanest, but also the most accurate. They have a knack, he explains, for zeroing in on what you don't like about yourself. He then quotes one mocking his "womanly hips." Mulaney pretends to be offended, but he's actually impressed at how precise the kids are.

If there's a topic near and dear to John Mulaney, it's making fun of John Mulaney. "When people make fun of me, I deserve it," he says. "If you're ever on the highway behind me, I hear you honking, and I also don't want me to be doing what I'm doing," he admits. "I don't like that I'm in that lane either."

Mulaney so loves making fun of himself that he even invited comedian friends Dan Mintz and Anthony Jeselink to record a commentary track relentlessly mocking his dated references to *Home Alone 2*. As much as his awkward demeanor, nervous energy and overall feebleness make it hard for him to get by, one senses that Mulaney is happy he's so hapless. It gives him more to work with. And Mulaney has a sizeable comedic arsenal for the war he wages on himself.

Most obviously, there's his distinctive voice and speaking pattern; he talks in a clipped, staccato rhythm with a heavy emphasis on the end of phrases. It naturally gives his set a forceful momentum and provides even his most rambling moments a sense of build. He can get a full head of steam going with a manic build-up (an out-of-control party he attended) and then stop hard on the punchline (how drinking a bottle of perfume was a sign he needed to quit drinking); the resulting 60-to-0 crunch gives the material a strange, offbeat feel that makes it even funnier. He also imitates Ice-T and a homeless gay man better than you would think and has a predilection for old-timey references, channeling 1930s-era gangsters or punctuating a joke about his airhead behavior with a Little Orphan Annie voice.

One of Mulaney's primary conceits is that he likes to point out unspeakably mundane things with zero notice, which is not funny in and of itself, but his process makes it more hilarious than it probably should be. He will stop at an odd moment in a sentence and pivot away, raising his voice to signify a robust conviction in the rightness of his vision, usually centered on a pedestrian observation. It helps reinforce the feeling that Mulaney was born without the tool kit most people have and has had to work at understanding how the world functions, and thus he sometimes gets too excited—or at least acts that way—when he makes connections others take for granted. (Many actually feel this way; that Mulaney is able to tap into this private emotion so well goes a long way in explaining his success.) Which is all a high-faulting way of explaining why he'll say, "So I lied...like a liar!" or point out that a 13-year-old is just a slightly older child, and it will kill.

Mulaney spends much of *New in Town* explaining why he is the way he is, from his high-strung parents (his mom told him about the death of Princess Diana in a distraught tone that led him to believe she thought he might

14

be responsible), childhood mockery (I won't ruin his best joke, but the part with the gong really makes you feel bad for him) and low self-esteem ("Before I had a girlfriend, I had no standard for how I should be treated as a human being. You could do anything to me. I was like a young Motown singer. I was just shiny and dumb and easy to trick."). To his credit, he rarely overplays the sympathy card, though sometimes his I'm-so-feeble gestures read as "Aren't I so cute?," a tic of which he should be wary.

As a joke writer, he's smart enough to layer in the underlying theme of his exasperation with himself throughout the set, but Mulaney drifts away from it enough to keep *Town* from becoming one-note. Riffing on how stupid pop culture can be is Joke Writing 101, but Mulaney zeroes in on details most would ignore for his critiques. He also tends to pick targets that are absurdly past their sell-by dates (*Home Alone 2*, *Def Comedy Jam*) or so middlebrow as to rarely attract much satire. Even people who don't watch *Law & Order: Special Victims Unit* will agree that after 11 years on the job, Ice-T shouldn't be surprised by the things perverts do, nor should he require a lengthy explanation of sex addiction.

Mulaney ultimately mocks himself so thoroughly that he seems simultaneously both egoless and self-inflating. Perhaps it's hard to be humble when you're such prime subject material.

January 29, 2012

Colin Quinn: *Long Story Short*
The Wilbur Theatre
Sunday, January 29, 2012

By Nick A. Zaino III

With *Long Story Short*, Colin Quinn has found the perfect vehicle to showcase the way his comic brain works. There is a theme and even a set with giant stone steps and a screen that cycles through the globe on musical cues to illustrate the next subject. He doesn't have to worry as much about winning the crowd over—they are there to hear his view of history, from the beginning. It also imposes just enough of a structure to keep Quinn on course while allowing him to ramble and free-associate in strategic places. And, as his Magners Comedy Festival evening proved, it gives him a show that can grow and change with current events. It's something he could do almost indefinitely, and probably should.

Going by the DVD chapter titles from the HBO special of the same name, one might think the current live show was basically the same as the special, and probably the same as the Broadway show (directed by Jerry Seinfeld) that preceded it. The story starts at "Survival of the Fittest" then bounces around the globe, keeping to a certain chronology. Quinn works his way from the ancient Greeks and Romans to the Silk Road and through Russia, Africa, China and America before winding up in Canada, the one place left in the world that's still beautiful. Of course, he notes, no one wants to stay there. Immigrants on their way to America come through Canada, see that it has jobs and social services, and still say, "I'll take my chances in that giant Ruby Tuesdays."

The "Ruby Tuesdays" line is a holdover from the HBO special. But instead of America being Canada's sloppy alcoholic brother who spills his drink all over the Gulf of Mexico, Canada is now Emilio Estevez to America's Charlie Sheen. It's a slight change, but Quinn has the opportunity to do that with a lot of different bits in the show, so even with multiple viewings there are still surprises.

He has a little leeway in his introduction as well. Quinn can choose a different jumping-off point to go back to the beginning; at the Wilbur he started with a bad, pandering Super Bowl joke about how he would come back next Sunday (Super Bowl Sunday, when the Pats would face the Giants) if the show went well. "Big Super Bowl joke," he grumbled. "Really went well." The joke didn't work, but his sarcasm and self-deprecation served as a nice ice breaker before he dove into the heavy stuff. He then used the possibility that 2012 might be the end of history (depending how one interprets the Mayan calendar) to get into the meat of the show.

Quinn's basic premise is that despite all our technological advances, humanity is basically the same. That's why we have nanotechnology but still need zoo guards to prevent people from jumping into the polar bear cage to get on YouTube. Why don't we get along? Because we're all "the descendents of the pricks." Our ancestors weren't the ones who waited politely and shared. They stole and killed while everyone else died. "We're not the 'After You's," says Quinn. "We're the 'After Me's."

17

True, large chunks of the show are the same. And necessarily so, since there are specific guideposts and a structured frame. For example, Quinn tells a story near the beginning about visiting his aunt in the hospital. As she was living out her last days, Quinn's family was busy complaining about the family from the next bed over stealing one of their chairs. He similarly relates how people can't even get along standing in line at the ATM. The premise is from the original show, but Quinn deviates again to describe how if someone takes a little too long with their transaction, a tribe starts to form amongst the people in line who have to decide what to do about it.

Even if some parts of the show are repeated verbatim, a lot of the concepts are pretty durable, and they hold up to repeated listenings while Quinn is getting to something new. And the ending is the best part, in which Quinn compares global politics to a bar fight and every country is a different barroom stereotype. It was his starting point when he built the show, and he worked backwards from there. Iraq is in the parking lot mouthing off, and everyone wants America to go talk to him. Iran is the guy who's a little slight but everyone's afraid of him anyway, standing there in his leisure suit drinking ginger ale. Of course it ends badly, and America winds up giving Greece a ride home and having a heart-to-heart about the trials of being an empire. It brings the whole show full circle, closing cleanly on a good punchline, one Quinn probably will never need to change.

January 30, 2012

Baratunde Thurston
How to Be Black
Harper

By Nick A. Zaino III

For those wondering about the title of Baratunde Thurston's
How to Be Black, Thurston is not offering to serve as Richard
Pryor to the reader's Gene Wilder in a *Silver Streak*-like
transformation. Readers who are not already black will find
no detailed instruction here on changing their pigment,
making them seem cooler at parties or justifying their love of
Avenging Disco Godfather (particularly as there is no
justification needed for loving *Avenging Disco Godfather*).

What Thurston intends to do with his debut book is
explain the black experience in America based on his own
experiences as well as those of experts on "The Black Panel,"
a group he has assembled purely for this purpose. While that
may not sound like a terribly funny premise, *Black* is only
partially a humor book. Thurston's comedy has been political
since his early days in Boston; as he notes in *Black*'s
Afterword, "While I definitely intend for it to be funny, there
is a message in it."

Much of *Black* is devoted to memoir, containing
moments both inspiring and disquieting. Thurston's mother
raised him by herself, taking care to expose him to a variety
of cultures while also preserving his black identity. He
subsequently worked his ass off at several jobs to make his
way through Harvard. It's hard not to stop and reflect when
he describes visiting Senegal's Goree Island, where slaves

were once prepared for transport, and looking through a door that opens to a steep drop into the ocean where troublemakers were tossed to their deaths.

The bulk of the book remains satirical, but Thurston is smart to couch it so deeply in his own point of view and to personalize it with stories provided by comedians, musicians and writers on his Black Panel. Thurston explores the notion raised in the wake of Barack Obama's election that we are a "post-racial society"—still a difficult issue to approach. He does point out that comedy and satire help soften the conversation. But tone is enormously important, and Thurston's is an interesting approach.

Bouncing back and forth between personal stories and satire can knock the reader a bit off kilter. Yet somehow that enhances its effectiveness. Thurston ends the chapter "Being Black at Harvard" with a photo of his mother hugging him and crying with joy at his graduation. The next chapter is "How To Be The Black Employee," which begins with Thurston writing about his post-graduation job search. He then stops on a dime and pivots from memoir to satire, telling the hypothetical story of a new black employee while addressing the reader in second person.

The new employee was hired for two jobs: to be a research associate, and to be black. The second job is, of course, not explicit but definitely implied, and Thurston defines it as representing the black community, making the company seem diverse and not racist, and increasing the coolness of the office environment. The shift from the personal achieves the effect of making the humor seem deadpan. It is presented in no less earnest a tone than Thurston's story about Harvard, and it may take the brain a few paragraphs (or pages) to adjust. That dissonance can create a wonderful moment in which it seems Thurston is advocating these steps completely sans irony, and when the reader is then hit with something silly, the laughter is that much more satisfying.

Again, there are real messages Thurston wants to get across. In his chapter "How To Be The Angry Negro" he suggests prefacing the answer to every question with, "As a black man," or "As a black woman," even if the question is "Paper or plastic?" When entering an elevator with a white person, he says the prospective Angry Negro might point out how "It wasn't long ago that people like me weren't allowed in this elevator. The good old days, huh?" Doesn't matter if the elevator was built last year. It still makes the white person uncomfortable, which is the point. The Angry Negro, he says, serves a function, but the chapter ends on a chilling note. "Remember that when people inevitably start to distance themselves from you," he writes. "Being hated is part of the job."

Thurston possesses chops as a standup, but this is not his act repackaged as a book. He has been writing humor as long as he has been performing, and he holds the title of Director of Digital at *The Onion*. He's actually more effective in print—where he has more time to put together a full package, to make his case and to provide context—than he is onstage. Thurston's a thoughtful guy, and when he says something that could potentially be considered inflammatory, there is always logic to it. Don't expect *Black* to be his last book.

January 31, 2012

21

Patrice O'Neal
Mr. P
BSeen Media

By Patrick Bromley

It's difficult to accept that, barring some sort of cynical cash-in, the stand-up album *Mr. P* is the last comedy the world is going to get from the late, great Patrice O'Neal. Arguably one of the best of his generation, the comic, who died last November following a stroke and long hospitalization, never quite achieved the mainstream success enjoyed by several of his contemporaries. Even if O'Neal hadn't passed away in late 2011, his posthumous release probably wouldn't have changed that reputation. It's perhaps too unstructured, moving too much in fits and starts—a better representation of how O'Neal worked than of how funny he was, and that's the kind of thing that appeals greatly to other comics but which has the potential to leave some audiences less than fully satisfied.

 Mr. P showcases nearly all of O'Neal strengths as a comic: his bruising honesty, his singular take on male-female relationships, his loose, open rapport with the audience and near-incomparable ability to turn unrehearsed crowd work into long-form stretches of inspired improvised comedy. So many contemporary comedians are compared to greats like Richard Pryor or Redd Foxx, but O'Neal is one of the few who actually deserves to be mentioned in the same sentence. He was the best kind of comic—the kind with a very specific, well-defined worldview—and there's no material on this last album that could be confused with any other comic's.

The record addresses politics without ever being overtly political. He brilliantly takes down the institution of the president, the election of Obama (whose only purpose, he purports, was to make everyone stop hating Bush), the class gap and the great appeal of wealth; it's observational in nature without ever lapsing into the same tired "Did you ever notice?" shtick that has given that particular style of comedy such a bad name. Even those tried and true topics that O'Neal tackles feel fresh because he approaches them from an angle that's never been covered, and his complete lack of ego or filter doesn't just stop him from saying the things he shouldn't—it practically compels him to. His material on the differences between black women and white women (which, yes, sounds hacky on paper but as delivered by O'Neal is anything but) feels honest and true even when it's not completely relatable. It's one of O'Neal's gifts—his material always rings true because it's totally genuine. There's no need to go for shock-value laughs even when what he's saying could be considered shocking, especially by more prudish listeners (who, for the record, have no business listening to a Patrice O'Neal record in the first place). Extended bits on government reparations and fighting between races feel dangerous and edgy not because O'Neal is cynically trying to push buttons, but because they truly represent how he looks at the world. One of his greatest strengths has always been his complete inability to pull punches, and *Mr. P* follows suit. In doing so, O'Neal is able to bring the audience to some places they might not otherwise be willing to go. He's convincing. He makes a good case. Mostly, though, he gets them on his side because he's hysterically funny, and it's better to be laughed with than laughed at.

The album feels in need of some editing at times; there are bits that O'Neal seems to be working out on stage as he goes through them, and which could have used some refining to sharpen them up. It's difficult to speculate whether or not, had he lived, O'Neal would have been involved in shaping some of what appears on the album (which was planned before his death, but only announced afterwards) into leaner, tighter chunks. But even the finished product presented as is gives a real sense of a Patrice O'Neal live show, from the crowd interactions to the improvised feel of his act to the pacing, which suggests that some thoughts are still in the writing stage. It lacks polish, to be sure, but there's a work-in-progress feel to *Mr. P* that will most definitely appeal to diehard comedy nerds.

This is not the release for which Patrice O'Neal will be remembered (that will more likely be *Elephant in the Room*, his 2011 Comedy Central stand-up special), but it is a good representation of him as a comic. *Mr. P* simply presents O'Neal as he was: a guy who didn't always need the sharpest, most well-rehearsed material, because he had a talent that even some of his more successful peers lack of just getting up on stage and being *so fucking funny*. It's a bit loose, a bit messy, but *Mr. P* is a fitting tribute to one of the best comics of the last 20 years. He will be missed.

February 6, 2012

Ron Funches
The Oriental Theater
Saturday, February 18, 2012

By John Wenzel

Ron Funches could easily build an act around his appearance, as many black and/or overweight comedians do. Or his current home of Portland, Oregon, a hipster haven that's recently achieved mainstream cachet with Fred Armisen and Carrie Brownstein's *Portlandia.* And while Funches, like any savvy, mostly unknown comedian, does exploit these facts to his advantage—see his rapturously-received *Conan* debut from August—he wisely avoids basing his persona on them. That's refreshing enough, given the fact that even casual audiences have grown so sophisticated as to expect more from their comics.

But he goes a step further, dispensing with the physical and situational jokes to focus on quiet absurdities, masterful pauses and, yes, the theme song from *Muppet Babies.* This is part of what has made Funches a presence at SF Sketchfest and Portland's Bridgetown Comedy Festival, as well as casting him as a young voice whose promise actually matches his current skills.

Funches made his Denver debut headlining the stately, aging Oriental Theater as part of local promoter Onus Spears's recurring *Huge Comedy Show.* Funches came out swinging with a jab at Spears's awkward emceeing and a recycled tweet comparing Colorado's arid landscape to the video game *Red Dead Redemption.* He led with the killer material from his *Conan* set, including his teenage move from the South Side of Chicago to Portland, and the fact that you can't put "allergic to energy" on a medical-marijuana application. (That, unsurprisingly, went over well in Denver's dispensary-choked environs.) Having personally heard those jokes live several times over the past 12 months, it was encouraging to see him tease them out on stage, adding languid but devastating codas and sentiments that trailed off so sublimely you could practically see the ellipses falling from his mouth.

Funches lacks physical spontaneity, preferring to swing his head gently from side to side with one hand stuffed in his pocket. And as a black man wearing dark clothes against a black curtain he threatened to fade into the background, despite the best efforts of the spotlight operator. Of course that made his occasional bursts of volume and cursing all the more notable. Like *Saturday Night Live* writer and mostly-clean comic John Mulaney (or, for that matter, Jim Gaffigan or Brian Regan), their judicious use underscored the bits far more effectively than a mindless onslaught of hoarsely-rendered profanity.

The most inspired moment came when he sang the theme to Eighties Saturday-morning cartoon *Muppet Babies.* "Some people don't know the Muppet Babies," he said, his tone simultaneously lamenting and marveling. "Everybody knows the Muppets. They fucked and had babies. They were given a show." He then contrasted the sweetness of the song's first verse—"We make our dreams come true / We'll do the same for you"—with the sinister implications of the second verse: "When your room looks kinda weird and you wish that you weren't there / Just close your eyes and make believe, and you can be anywhere." "That's pretty fucked up," he finished. "I told my son, 'If your room looks messed up and you wish that you weren't there, do not make believe. Call Children's Services. Daddy has made an error of some kind."

Like the oft-imitated Mitch Hedberg, the laughs came less from the material (though Hedberg's was often brilliant, too) than the offbeat emphasis Funches placed on the syllables. He reinforced that with a bit about his autistic son who knows only about 30 words, his favorite three of which are "more," "pancakes" and "bee-yotch!" It's a rhythm familiar to all standups: setup, slow build, violent release. But Funches illustrated it physically with a joke that took almost half the night to quietly prepare. He started with a factoid he'd recently read that "Forty percent of all American cats are obese…which is great news if you love fat pussy. SKITTLES!" From his formerly pocket-stuffed hand dozens of multicolored candies flew in a haphazard arc toward the shocked audience. Now that's commitment to a joke.

Agreeable but not always galvanizing, the rest of the set included a sung bit (the clap-along rap he composed with his son, "Oreos and Bacon") and conventional but funny riffs on neck tattoos, the Discovery Channel and psychedelic mushrooms. He ended by bringing two female volunteers on stage for an impromptu "game show," the categories/only answers for which were "Shitty, Really Shitty and Really About Shit." The prize? "For one week and one week only I will put you on top of my masturbation Rolodex." Cue groans, laughter and applause.

The crowd was already his, but he made a point to thank them: "You guys are a good audience. That's hard to fuck up around." True, but it remains to be seen how Funches fares with random club audiences as he continues to

27

break away from the comedy insiders and hipsters who have embraced him so far.

February 20, 2012

Sara Benincasa
Agorafabulous!: Dispatches From My Bedroom
William Morrow

By Nick A. Zaino III

It's an enormous tribute to Sara Benincasa as a writer and a comedian that there is anything at all to laugh at in her memoir *Agorafabulous!: Dispatches From My Bedroom.* Any thought that this will be a light-hearted romp through some minor neuroses is dashed on page two in an Introduction in which Benincasa recounts the truly horrific suicide of a high-school classmate. He was a seemingly perfect kid and no one saw it coming, least of all Benincasa.

It's an ideal place to start her story, a tale of coming of age and conquering fear. It foreshadows the seriousness of Benincasa's impending agoraphobia and highlights her outsider status. She would have difficulty coming to terms with both afflictions as she worked her way through different colleges and career paths. But to find her place, she had to first be willing to leave her bed.

Benincasa provides an inventory of her fears right up front in list form, including the severity, whether or not she is currently over it and what the solution was. She has overcome her fear of having a wet head, for example, and did this by "Avoiding the shower; using a high-power hair dryer with a diffuser for less frizz and extra curls." She is mostly over her fear of leaving the house, thanks to Prozac, Xanax, Klonopin, therapy and a stuffed giraffe that accompanies her everywhere. She is not yet over her fear of God but is working on it by "Consorting with atheists and other hell-bound types, like comedians."

Benincasa writes about debilitating panic attacks and how, when she should have been having the time of her life in college, she decided she was an incurable freak, "designed not to be displayed and celebrated but to be hidden in the darkness, an ugly, stinking waste of flesh." The first big warning sign came during her senior year of high school and a class trip to Sicily, when she had a panic attack and was rushed to the nearest hospital. This was partially brought on by the mean, popular girls who tortured her, and whom Benincasa skewers here. But she gets to meet "Dr. Sophia Loren" and her bevy of hot assistants in the socialist hospital, is given drugs that make it fun to linger on consonants at the end of phrases, and all returns to normal.

The normality doesn't last. In college at Emerson, she becomes afraid to leave her apartment. Then she becomes afraid to use her bathroom, and then to leave her bed. She stops eating, because eating leads to energy and energy to wanting to do things, which might lead to leaving her apartment. She uses cereal bowls for a toilet, hiding them under her bed and in her closet. She expects to die, even hopes for it. Thanks to friends, Benincasa is forced to leave the apartment, and she returns home to New Jersey for therapy.

The word "journey" is overused these days. It's applied to contestants who have spent three weeks on *The Bachelor* and to just about anyone who is not dead (and some who are) to describe how they attained their current status. But what Benincasa goes through in *Agorafabulous!* can fairly be described as a journey worthy of Ulysses. It takes her from Jersey to Boston to Texas to New York, from peeing in bowls in her apartment to performing stand-up comedy in front of hundreds of people at a time. Along the way she faces a rabid Santa Claus doppelganger outside a Planned Parenthood, the deranged leader of a retreat in Pennsylvania and catty high schoolers, and finds friends who act as guardian angels.

Somewhere on that path, Benincasa became extremely self-aware and began writing about her neuroses and character flaws with impressive clarity and humor. There are no gags in this book. The humor flows from the details, tragic as they sometimes are. The single thing that would calm Benincasa when she had her college attack was listening to the Dave Matthews Band's "Satellite" on a constant loop, which was fine when she was alone, but less so when her mother was driving her home. Later, sitting despondent in a hospital after a break up, Benincasa realizes she's not crazy, just broken-hearted, and is able to lift her spirits with chicken soup and Liz Phair's "Fuck and Run."

The ultimate epiphany comes in the form of stand-up comedy. Benincasa thinks she has finally achieved her dream when she enters teaching college at Columbia, but on the suggestion of a classmate finds her true calling making people laugh. In a refreshing twist, comedy is the final step toward sanity. It gives Benincasa's life direction and purpose and helps her feel whole. *Agorafabulous!* is proof she has found her place.

February 23, 2012

Garfunkel and Oates
Slippery When Moist
Self-Released

By Steve Heisler

The deck is stacked against musical comedy—an act born,
more than anything, out of a need for novelty. There are
plenty of examples of musical comedy gone horribly wrong;
for every Flight of the Conchords, there are countless open
mic-ing duos, possibly from New Zealand, rapping about
how "It's Business Timeframe." As the forever popular site
StuffWhitePeopleLike.com put it: "…when you have jokes that
aren't that great and music that isn't that great, you can mix
them together and create something that will entertain white
people."

But it can be good. Seriously! The secret is to infuse
the comedy with music's best elements. In the theatrical
sense, characters burst into song when mere words can no
longer express what they're feeling inside. Popular musical
comedy acts like Reggie Watts, Hard 'N' Phirm and
occasionally Garfunkel and Oates couch extreme, silly and
occasionally off-putting sentiments through the natural
evolution of the music. As each song develops, so does the
comedic point of view, building surprises in along the way.

I say "occasionally" when talking about G&O—a duo
comprised of Kate Micucci and Riki Lindhome—because
while they're capable of this magical and elusive synergy,
there's little of that on *Slippery When Moist*. Their song "Sex
With Ducks," off last year's *All Over Your Face*, disguised a

pro-gay rights message inside a sweet, harmonized song that got more lyrically ridiculous as it went on (as nods to the TV show *Duck Tales* are wont to do). There are a handful of examples on *Moist*, but mostly the album has no build, no novelty and barely any harmony. Tracks merely involve Micucci and Lindhome expressing the same sentiment over and over again...through *song*!

Though it's cycled the internet since November 2010, "Handjob, Blandjob, I Don't Understand Job" is the poster song for one of *Moist*'s biggest problems: cleverness for the sake of cleverness. The track is about how Micucci and Lindhome never learned how to give a proper handjob, and how awkward it is to have that "lesson" in adulthood. The two trade couplets, describing how their nerdy adolescences involved zero penises in their hands. Then, rather than delve further into those recollections, the two abandon the song's foundation and start trying to out-clever one another in describing the penis itself. "The top is the part that confuses me the most / It looks like a Silly Putty Pac-Man ghost," raps Lindhome, followed by Micucci comparing the balls to the two critics on *The Muppet Show*. There's nothing wrong with this imagery in and of itself; it's actually quite inventive. It's just that the rest of the song establishes an element of story, and before it develops, the song is over. Same with "Go Kart Racing" and "Google"—songs about accidental masturbation and internet-stalking dates, respectively, that get their jokes out in the first chorus and can't quite find any new footing after that.

Moist's simplest songs are the most successful. On "Silver Lining" the pair speak directly to a woman who's been soured by a bad break up. "If he never felt that way / Why would you want him to stay?" is perhaps the most subtle line

33

of the song, but any tune with the chorus, "Get up out of bed / Right foot, left foot, moving" isn't trying to be deft. Plus it comes after a seven-second track called "The Ex-Boyfriend Song" that literally just says, "I fucking hate you, you fucking liar." The bluntness of "Silver Lining" is its best asset, though; it's clear and concise, not wasting precious seconds with superfluous details or slick-though-out-of-place imagery. (When an album only totals 24 minutes, every word counts.) "My Apartment's Very Clean Without You" is the other side of the coin: The duo sings from the perspective of "Silver Lining"'s target, about how lonely and quiet—but clean—singledom can be. There's a sweet, deliberate build to the song, methodically adding details until the title itself shifts ever-so-slightly into vulnerable territory. It's also the only track that involves any sort of vocal harmony, which is a shame since both women have really nice voices.

G&O don't have to be funny to be meaningful. "Save The Rich," their ode to the Occupy Wall Street movement, says more in the lyric "Save the rich / By doing nothing at all" than it does in the witty recitations of the One Percent's platitudes, like shipping jobs overseas. "I Would Never (Have Sex With You)" would be a fine ode to platonic friendship if it wasn't immediately followed by "I Would Never (Dissect A Ewe)," which is the same song, just full of science-y terms. *Slippery When Moist* too often swaps out comedic catharsis for cleverness, especially the plethora of "See what we did there?" moments. And given there's music too, a medium built on catharsis, it's all the more noticeable.

February 28, 2012

34

David Koechner
Empire Comedy
Saturday, March 4, 2012

By Josh Bell

David Koechner may not be the ideal performer to entertain a full Vegas lounge. The Empire Comedy audience at Paris Las Vegas seemed a little baffled by Koechner's sometimes nearly avant-garde act, especially following the two fairly standard local comics who warmed up the crowd. Having received formal improv training with ImprovOlympic and Second City troupes as opposed to years of working the stand-up stage, Koechner is best known for his roles in mainstream comedy movies (*Anchorman*, *Talladega Nights*) and sitcoms (*The Office*), so his off-kilter and esoteric performance—a mix of traditional stand up, storytelling and sketches—may have caught attendees off guard at first.

After making a few jokes about his "Hey, it's that guy!" character-actor status ("He just realized who it was," Koechner said of a confused patron, then speculated that people might think he was *The Daily Show* correspondent Rob Corddry or *That '70s Show* father Kurtwood Smith) and the requisite Vegas references (including brief impressions of Celine Dion and *Jersey Boys*), Koechner launched into a long, meandering story about returning to his tiny Missouri hometown for what he thought was the chance to be the grand marshal in an annual parade. It was the sort of personality-enhancing anecdote one might expect to hear on a late-night talk show, but it featured no punchlines and elicited no laughter.

The tale was kind of engrossing in its mundanity, though, and Koechner never faltered in the telling, even when he seemed to be losing momentum. Despite the tepid response, Koechner clearly didn't alienate them entirely, and anytime he responded to questions or comments, he was engaged and sharp. One gentleman with a thick Southern accent completely derailed Koechner's next long narrative in a thoroughly entertaining way: after a bit about a homeless guy offering to show Koechner his balls for five dollars, the boisterous exhibitionist yelled out that he'd gladly show Koechner (and the entire room) his own testicles for free, and Koechner brought him onstage to go through with it before security put the brakes on the whole endeavor.

Riffing on the eager ball-shower (who did not back down from his offer) put Koechner back on the crowd's good side, as did his jokes about the passersby peering in the lounge's large windows to get a look at what was going on inside. And it was a good thing that he could take time for that interaction, since subsequent bits about Socrates, Paul Lynde and Rush Limbaugh appeared to sail right over most heads. Even a seemingly standard chunk about Koechner parenting his five kids veered off into odd territory, as he sang what he said was his favorite nursery rhyme for the kids, which involved encouraging them to become hobos.

Things then got even weirder. Right in the middle of his parenting chunk Koechner abruptly put on a fat suit and wig to segue into a very long segment as Roy, a 350-pound gay man. The majority didn't really know what to make of Roy, but like everything in Koechner's act, the character inhabited a fully-realized world of his own. Koechner as Roy

36

told a story at least as long and rambling as his hometown-parade account, only way more bizarre. It involved Roy, the latest *Twilight* movie and a briefcase full of movie-theater snacks, and it only grew funnier the stranger and more off-putting it got.

Then just as quickly, Koechner took off his fat suit and jumped right back into material about his kids without even missing a beat. At some point a good portion of the audience must have ended up on Koechner's wavelength, and by the time he changed outfits again to close out the show as his long-running alter ego Gerald "T-Bones" Tibbons (along with Dave "Gruber" Allen, the Largo regulars were invited to open for Tenacious D and best remembered from 2007's *The Naked Trucker and T-Bones Show* on Comedy Central), the laughs were much more forthcoming. It helped that ignorant redneck T-Bones is an easier persona than Roy for folks to wrap their heads around, and that much of Koechner's T-Bones bit consisted of singing catchy, funny parody songs.

Aided by a couple of musicians from the lounge's house band, he sang a psychedelic ode to T-Bones's lost father, astronaut Buzz Aldrin, and then ended the set with the rousing blues number "Two Dollars and a Hand Job," which got everyone singing along. It was exactly the kind of dumb fun that was probably expected from Koechner in the first place, but it somehow felt more cathartic after the difficult (but rewarding, for the right people) material that preceded it. Maybe Koechner was an odd fit for a casino lounge, but he ultimately managed to make it work.

March 5, 2012

Ralphie May
Too Big to Ignore
Comedy Central

By Michael Tedder

There is much more to Ralphie May than his size, but the man did name his most recent stand-up special *Too Big to Ignore*, so it behooves us to tackle the subject up front. An excellent mimic who would have done gangbusters in the silent-film era, May knows how to use his weight as a physical prop, and is particularly fond of bugging his eyes out beyond the limits of his face before retreating them back to the point where they almost disappear into his ample folds of flesh. He seems to weld his jowls like a muscle; one suspects he purposefully makes them waddle at just the right level of excitement to complement his main three facial expressions, the "Can you believe this shit?," the "For real, can you believe this shit?" and, every so often, the classic "What the shit?"

His girth also has subtext. May is too smart to say it forthrightly, but as someone who grew up severely overweight, he knows what it is like to be viewed as different. This has, thankfully, not embittered him. Even at his most frustrated, he practically sweats joy. When May talks about his wife and kids or thanks the audience for continuing to support him, it's clear he's still surprised at how good he now has it. His experiences as an obese man have given him sympathy for those who continue to experience prejudice.

May is a great humanist, fighting for the dignity of all people with the crassest jokes possible.

Because he knows what it's like to get endless shit just for being who you are—and because he clearly doesn't have a hateful bone in his ample body—May believes he has license to say whatever he wants…which is often the sort of filth that merits as many "Oh my God!"s as actual laughter. There's a bit where poor May is dragged to the mall, even though "Nothing there fits me except for socks," and his family enters an elevator with two "smoking hot" *America's Next Top Model* contestants. ("So hot, I was stunned honest. If my wife had asked me, I would have to tell her the truth: 'I would bang both of them in front of your family.'") After noting one's G-string placement, he observes the other model's particularly tight pants and develops a case of one of the most immature Tourette's possible, invoking the phrase "fat monkey" until it becomes a mantra. When his son grabs said monkey (May admits he could have stopped him, but "Can't c-block your own son!"), the model questions May's parenting technique and eventually his girth, to which he replies, "Yes, I'm fat. But notice: loose clothing. That thing is like a catfish that's been out of water too long." (His suffocating-catfish face is simply too beautifully weird to accurately describe.)

May has an outspoken political streak, one welcome in a stand-up era that has become generally apolitical in recent years. But even when attacking prejudice, he does so with all the gleeful irreverence he brings to G-string jokes. He often seems like a real-life Eric Cartman, only knowingly flirting with close-minded ideas in order to shed light on their idiocy. Which is another way of saying that there's a part where he sings "The Muslim is Going to Get You" to the tune of Gloria Estefan's "Rhythm Is Gonna Get You," mocking the fears of White America by rubbing their faces in it: "Last thing you'll smell is couscous, camel hump and diesel fuel." Though May takes his get-away-with-whatever persona a bit too far, a screed against declining blowjob quality is the only part of the set that actually feels ugly and unearned. He could also do with about 30 percent less use of the word "bitch."

May takes down Arizona's immigration laws (getting interrogated for "driving while Mexican" or just mowing your own lawn) and the gays-in-the-military debate, stances greeted with an implied "Of course. Everybody thinks that; don't be so proud of yourself." Yet when May talks about how he escaped the small-town minds of his native Arkansas, there's a sense that many of his viewpoints are hard-won victories earned from relentless introspection, and something he probably still has to justify to people in his life. He'll throw these people a bone with knocks against the Prius ("the gayest car") before going in on homophobia, praising gay men for taking competition out of dating pool, and eventually coming to the conclusion that if straight people don't like gay people, it's their fault for making more gay people. (No amount of lesbian donut-bumping, he tactfully points out, will result in more lesbians.) To May the more gay people born and Mexicans in this country, the better, as long as they aren't easily offended by dirty jokes. Seems the biggest thing about him is his heart.

March 6, 2012

Doug Stanhope
Before Turning the Gun on Himself…
Roadrunner Records

By John Wenzel

The morbid title of Doug Stanhope's latest is enough to drive away anyone who might be offended by the actual material—and enough to attract the stereotypically sullen, nihilist, bitterly alcoholic curmudgeons who have supported Stanhope's career thus far. What else to expect from a man who's spent a good chunk of his time celebrating drugs and railing against buttoned-down idiocy?

That's obviously a bit reductive. But shock and filth are less valuable commodities than they used to be, especially in comedy, so it's reassuring that Stanhope's virulently anti-bullshit stances have remained transgressive with each new album, even as the ravages of partying have continued to turn his voice to asthmatic gravel.

He opens with a self-effacing bit about how shitty he looks in the mirror these days, which inevitably leads to introspection and a comment on the late Mitch Hedberg. "Drugs killed him, but they didn't ruin his life by any stretch," he says earnestly. That's certainly debatable, but Stanhope at least turns it funny, noting how Hedberg's family started a charity golf tournament to support a rehab facility in his honor—which he says is akin to the family of a guy who died during the Olympics holding a charity pie-eating contest to keep kids away from sports.

Stanhope spits furiously about "the cottage-industry fraud" that is rehab and reserves particular scorn for Dr. Drew Pinsky of *Celebrity Rehab* and *Loveline* fame: "Just hearing his name, bile comes out of me." When Stanhope recites his grievances against Pinsky, the bottomless apoplexy is almost comforting. Passion makes him more articulate and able to walk the ever-thinning line between entertainment and angry screed. The name of the bit? "Dr. Drew Is to Medicine What David Blaine Is to Science." Spot on, vicious and hilarious. All nine minutes of it.

Track names read like punk-rock song titles, and everything implied is eventually laid out. In fact, "My Piss Stinks" includes an improbably detailed discussion of the consistency of his feces.

The Salt Lake City crowd, for the most part, is adoring but sedate. And since Stanhope seems to take special pleasure in performing in risky environments, there's palpable tension when he asks offended audience members to leave.

Some comics carefully weigh the specific over the relatable, but Stanhope goes all in, using particular cities, brand names and animals to make his points (yes, he has clearly mastered the use of nouns). He celebrates drunkenness, but uses his salty intelligence and vocabulary to pull it off. If you're not already on his shaky, pro-Charlie Sheen wavelength, it comes off as the rant of a college freshman using the old "It's a free country!" cry to justify any number of despicable behaviors.

That said, Stanhope's effectiveness lies in both his grasp of the big picture and his willingness to spit out facts in service of a joke. "The average cost in this country of raising a single child to the age of 17 is now $227,000," he quotes, taking down the hypocrisy of people who bitch about the economy while continuing to squeeze out kids. He's also That Guy who defends liberal use of the words "faggot" and "nigger" by attempting to strip them of societal context and apply his own.

The rest of the set doesn't so much evolve as bob up and down on a sea of anger. Is he saying "faggot" slightly less? That means he's (relatively) calm. One gets the sense that about half the audience doesn't fully comprehend what he's talking about, instead sitting back and drunkenly clapping at his curse words and hoarse volume, cheering and wooing every time he talks in an exaggerated "black" voice. The tongue-twisting bit "Keynesian Economic Theory as Applied to Private Sector Independent Contracting" is delivered in the voice of a black prostitute who veers from talking about her "shit pussy" to Nobel-prize winning economist Milton Friedman. It's followed, appropriately, by a bit called "Giant Black Cock," in which Stanhope asks the audience to volunteer one for an impromptu after-show photo.

An hour long with 12 distinct tracks, *Before Turning the Gun on Himself…* feels overall economical, especially after last year's somewhat bloated *Oslo: Burning the Bridge to Nowhere*. The first three-quarters of *Before* are mostly bite-sized, self-contained jokes, whereas the last are each about 12 minutes. Bottom-heavy, to be sure.

What's both frustrating and fascinating about Stanhope is the paradox of his persona: the intelligent, lowbrow artist who hates intellectuals and artists. Yet one doesn't get the sense that he hates himself. He just hates people who talk without thinking.

But as he usually does, Stanhope effectively insulates himself from any criticisms by acknowledging them. His closing bit is even called "Remember When I Used to Give a Shit?" Of course he still does. He's just realized that it doesn't make everything that infuriates him go away.

March 8, 2012

Steve Martin
The Ten, Make That Nine, Habits of Very Organized People.   Make That Ten.
Grand Central Publishing

By Nick A. Zaino III

In his 2007 autobiography *Born Standing Up*, Steve Martin pinpointed the moment he knew his stand-up career was over. It was 1981, and he was playing Las Vegas. As he scanned the packed floor, he saw something he described as "so disturbing that I didn't mention it to my friends, my agent, or my manager." It was, in the back of the room, one booth with empty seats.

Then he played Atlantic City, and for third night in a row, the guitar that was supposed to descend from the rafters failed to do so. After the show, he was enraged, not at the prop, but at the fact that he'd lost touch with his art. "I never did stand-up again," he wrote.

With the success of *The Jerk*, Martin transitioned into movies, and down the road also became a playwright and novelist. He would still pop up on *Saturday Night Live*, on late-night talk shows, and made a couple of appearances as "The Great Flydini," a magician who pulls things from the fly of his pants. That was the main body of his live performing.

In 2010, Martin discovered Twitter. Martin's account, @SteveMartinToGo, might be the closest he ever comes to doing stand up again; it wasn't the same as being in a room with and performing for a live audience, but it did allow Martin to reach people in real time. He enjoyed it so much, his new book, *The Ten, Make That Nine, Habits of Very Organized People. Make That Ten.: The Tweets of Steve Martin*, is comprised of some of Martin's best tweets and the responses from his fans.

In the Introduction, Martin writes that he first started Twitter to promote his other projects. That didn't work out, but he got hooked on the connection to the fans. This is, after all, a guy who used to take his audiences out of the club to a McDonald's or a swimming pool after a show. He craves a creative challenge and enjoys interacting with his audience, two needs that were impossible to fill once he became famous.

Once he discarded it as a promotional tool, Martin was hooked on the comedy potential of Twitter: "I found the limits exciting, and liked that these thoughts popped up randomly on someone else's device, perhaps catching them at an odd moment." He was thrilled when he found out people were tweeting him back, but when they sometimes complained, it "would make me panic and sweat like I was a first-time comedian on an audition stage."

The book has the feel of a new comedian testing his abilities, and Martin acknowledges that. He tries one-liners, storylines, strings with a theme and photo tweets. Sometimes his audience outshines him, something that also seems to thrill him. A lot of comedians were quick to use Twitter to toss bons mots to their fans (and WitStream was quick to aggregate those posts). Many also tweet with their fans. And hashtags allowed a lot of people to join in and monitor trends.

Martin goes beyond all that. In one string, he starts a sing-along where his audience filled in the last line of different Christmas carols. He would pick his favorite, tweet the complete verse and move on to the next.

> That's right.
> "Don we now our gay, I mean stylish,
> red sweater." Fa la la la la, la la la la.
> Troll the ancient…?

In another, he tells the story of being on jury duty.

> REPORT FROM JURY DUTY:
> Defendants hair looking very
> Conan-y today. GUIILTY.

The one-liners tend to be absurd, very much in the vein of Martin's first book, *Cruel Shoes*. It might take a minute to discern what he was doing when he tweeted, ".I leef driew yadot." But when it does register, Martin's old stage voice comes ringing through.

At first, Martin tracked his responders as anonymous before finally starting to take note of their handles. Occasionally whole pages are devoted to Martin's fans, which is a little disappointing for a book of only 103 pages. Sometimes the responses are corny, but sometimes Martin's tweets are, too. And sometimes Martin almost seems like the straight man.

> @SteveMartinToGo:
> There's a rumor that a recent Oscar
> Host is going to play Catwoman.
> Waiting by my phone for the call.

@mattMICKenna:
Oh no, Steve, that was Anne
Hathaway. I see why you're confused though. You
have hosted the Oscars.

There is no doubt comedians will find different ways
to use Twitter as the technology evolves. It must be
gratifying to Martin that he found a way to present the new
technology in an old format. And it's amusing to think he
might draw an older audience onto Twitter once they see
how it works in print. But most of all, it's good to have more
immediate access to that comic mind once again.

March 9, 2012

Lewis Black
In God We Rust
Epix

By Steve Heisler

The words "Go fuck yourself!" are used as a punchline multiple times on *In God We Rust*, but it hardly gets old; Lewis Black has mastered its nuance. There's a special, subdued "Go fuck yourself!" reserved for a confusing review of his show in the *Wendover Times*. There's a powerful "Go fuck yourself!" targeted at whoever dropped Valentine's Day—the most depressing holiday for single people—smack dab in the middle of the already-most depressing month of the year. His "Go fuck yourself!"s about the Tea Party and Michelle Bachmann are aged with the bile of a 30-plus year career, spanning nine comedy albums, seven DVDs and three books (plus whatever the movie *Unaccompanied Minors* was).

Rage is the ballerina dance of Black's comedy, and on *In God We Rust*, it seethes mostly below the surface, bubbling up in those well-placed "Go fuck yourself!"s. Unfortunately the same fails to hold true much of anywhere else. Given how deliberate and measured Black builds his arguments and emotional palette, it's surprising when it's not followed by a big moment of catharsis, or even a sentiment at the end of the special that ties the disparate threads together. Though it doesn't come full circle, *In God We Rust* remains rife with pure Black observations on finding the absurdity in despair.

Take, for example, his thoughts on a terrorist in the news who armed his dick with explosives and hopped on a plane to Detroit. Why Detroit? Because the ticket was cheaper. This fact in and of itself could easily provide Black with fodder for another hour of comedy all together, but that would be an easy target. Instead, Black sets off for Democrats and Republicans, two groups he surmises are to blame *equally* for terrorist attacks. It took them eight and a half years, he says, to get a list of known terrorist suspects to our nation's airports after 9/11. "How long is eight and a half years?" he asks. "Imagine if your son or daughter came home after college, then didn't leave for *eight and a half years."* Then, to further demonstrate the incompetence of our government, he posits that he could have put those names on a bunch of duckie boats, sent them out to sea randomly on the Hudson River, and in eight and a half years one would have probably made its way to an airport somewhere.

The strength in that joke is just how far Black will go to make his point. It's not enough for him to call our government lazy; he constructs a whimsical and ridiculous scenario to further demonstrate just how lazy it is. Point being, when he gets going, there are few things in the comedy world as sound and entertaining as a Black rant.

One of the problems haunting *In God We Rust*, though, is that Black uses this power on seemingly inconsequential targets—inconsequential in that they're not tied to something larger than the joke itself. He spends a *great* deal of time talking about his phone, first the iPhone and the genital-less weirdos who work at the Apple store, then moving on to his Droid and the genital-full weirdos who work at the Verizon store. It's an articulate and detailed distillation of 21st-century frustration, but it continues far longer than necessary and ends more with a whimper than a bang. Meanwhile, other weighty topics are given the short shrift. Black mentions abortion during another part of his set, follows with a pause and notes that every time he says that word, he can hear everyone's "anus snap shut." This sort of setup implies we'll be here for a while, but a few lines later the topic is abandoned for a story about how he once hung out with Ringo Starr and winked at Paul McCartney.

Black's rhythm is slightly off on *Rust*. He speaks very slowly and allows plenty of room for audience reaction, and the space between jokes makes the sudden shifts in topic all the more jarring. There are a few points in his set, like the abortion/Ringo Starr segue, that particularly stand out, but Black is mostly in his groove. With about 10 minutes to go in his set, Black senses he's reached the home stretch and digs deep into the Tea Party (as well as *Farmville*). He actually pulls off the impressive feat of finding them downright admirable; if they can convince a bunch of poor, trailer-living folks to protest taxing the rich, he says, "*That's* leadership." He also sees a great deal of himself in the Tea Party. They're angry, in particular, and as he says in one of the most salient lines of the special, "If anybody knows anger, it's fuckin' moi." And when Black's right, he's oh so right.

March 20, 2012

51

Maria Bamford
Laughing Skull Lounge
Thursday, March 22, 2012

By Austin L. Ray

Calling Maria Bamford "one of a kind" feels cliché in such a staggering way that you can practically hear her strapping on one of her trademark voices—maybe the polished, hoity-toity character evoking a privileged, suburban lady of leisure who never had to left a finger in her life—to mock the very idea of it. It's true, however. Perhaps the best way of describing her fucking-with-the-form brand of oddball, voice-enhanced humor comes from the liner notes of the limited-edition set of mini-CDs released in 2006 for the second incarnation—Patton Oswalt, Brian Posehn, Bamford and Eugene Mirman—of the Comedians of Comedy tour: "She has a wonderful, clear speaking voice, but that's just how she sounds when she's making fun of boring, normal people."

Bamford is more than just a myriad of voices, though, despite that particular aspect of talent earning her considerable work. Her bits somehow remain coherent despite their seeming readiness to crumble at any moment, but it's all in the subtleties. For instance, she took to the Laughing Skull stage Thursday night spouting off obvious Atlanta references—Tyler Perry, the city's notable aquarium, the Braves—in an attempt to warm up the crowd, even though she'd already grabbed the attention of the nerds in the house by wearing a Beards of Comedy t-shirt. Likewise, when she's cycling through voices during lengthy bits, it's the way she stares terrifying daggers into the crowd or occasionally breaks just a little (which is rare), lighting up the room with a sly grin or a knowing smirk that really drives the point home.

But she utilizes her eccentricity, honing it into a precisely measured, mesmerizing tone that brings the audience into her world regardless of background or previous familiarity. Bamford gets those people in pocket to the point where a simple riff on too-happy folks and relationship "fights" which amount to "He doesn't like onions," totally kills. The line "He doesn't like onions," is not funny in and of itself, of course, not even in the context of the joke. It's a combination of her delivery and the ambience she creates with her very being that makes it work. If that sounds like some hippie shit, it's because Bamford is like a temporary, benevolent and harmless cult leader on stage—everything changes when she's up there.

Roughly three-fourths of Bamford's material was fresh stuff not frequently performed in recent years, and, when mixed with some classic bits she's been doing for a while, the set flowed nicely. She tore down celebrities like Paula Deen (her voice eventually morphing into some Dark Lord of the Underworld during the bit), Jennifer Aniston ("…a strong, sexy monkey who's going to tell me where all the bananas are located,") and The Macho Man (To someone in the front row, whose shirt was Randy Savage-themed: "How's he doing?"). She shook a finger at the secret, new-wavey Christians in her neighborhood who try to entice her with live music, coffee and youth-center culture, ultimately spurting out in frustration, "Stop lurking behind your Jimi Hendrix font!" But elsewhere she turned the focus on herself, talking about her earlier days as a shaved-head hippie playing music on the streets, eventually agreeing to "work for The Man," and then, later, saying exactly what The Man tells her to say. Was it a reference to her Target commercials? A particular, unnamed movie of which she's ashamed? It doesn't matter, frankly, as long as it pays her bills and keeps her doing stand up.

Another fitting explanation of Bamford's unique comedic stylings derives from one of her best jokes. While describing how she mentors neighborhood kids without anyone asking her to or even knowing she's doing so, she detailed a conversation with a young girl:

"My dad said you're a comedian. Tell me a joke," the child demands.
"It's not like that…" Bamford replies, petrified, her voice trailing off.
"How can you be a comedian if you can't tell me a joke?"
"Call my manager; he'll explain everything!" Bamford concludes, panicked.

At the risk of getting high-mindedly "What does it all mean?" about the state of comedy, it's worth reveling in this moment where Bamford basically lays out her modus operandi. This is a veteran comic who has no use for doing one-liners, traditional setup-punchline jokes or even avant-garde bits that only push the envelope slightly. Instead she inhabits her own little plane of comedic existence, and while it's probably pretty lonely there, the rewards for the people willing to listen are rich and weird, just like anything truly worth doing in life. "I have nothing of value!" she whisper-screamed at a hypothetical suitor in an older bit about her inability to accept people who are interested in her. Hopefully, she's in on that joke.

March 23, 2012

Moshe Kasher
Kasher in the Rye
Grand Central Publishing

By John Wenzel

The recent glut of comedy podcasts has obscured that other glut of comedians-talking-about-themselves-outside-of-stand-up outlet: the comedy book. And while we usually need another comedy podcast or book about as much as a well-placed hole in the cranium, any bracing, intelligent, funny entry is always welcome.

San Francisco-bred upstart Moshe Kasher's *Kasher in the Rye* is one of those: a briskly-paced, biting memoir of Kasher's troubled early years. And really, if these sordid events had happened to someone other than Kasher, he would still be a solid choice for a ghost writer. His breathless delivery and sweetly grim material have grabbed a good deal of attention with appearances on *Late Night With Jimmy Fallon* and *Chelsea Lately* while killing it at festivals and slowing climbing the oily rungs of the Hollywood ladder.

Kasher in the Rye goes a long way toward explaining the appeal of his prickly, no-bullshit stage presence. But while most comedy books are extensions of an act or a persona, *Kasher in the Rye* is a tale unto itself. In lesser hands it wouldn't shed much new light on substance abuse, lawlessness and mental instability. In Kasher's, the memories crackle and spark like a lit firecracker, always threatening to blow his fingers across the room.

The book jacket is careful to note that this is not "an 'eye opener' to the horrors of addiction," but one would be forgiven for gleaning that from the flashy subtitle: *The True Tale of a White Boy from Oakland Who Became a Drug Addict, Criminal, Mental Patient, and Then Turned 16*. Early on Kasher writes, "You'll be shocked to realize that a drug-addicted, mentally ill journey of violent insanity is a bit of a hazy cat's-cradle to untangle," effectively offering an anti-James Frey disclaimer for the accuracy of the events. It's not needed. You can't make most of this shit up, as they say, and wouldn't want to if you could.

There are no spoilers in going over the basics: Kasher was born to deaf parents, which instantly contributed to his sense of *otherness*. His mother stole him away from his father to move to Oakland, and at the tender age of 4 his "feral" behavior landed him in anger-related therapy. He struggled with his family's Judaism. He adopted a fearless, jokey attitude to get by in Oakland's brutal public-school system. He stole smokes and ran with kids from broken homes, escaping reality with weed and Everclear and phone sex before moving onto tagging and acid dealing. He got into trouble with cops and landed in more therapy and mental institutions. You get the picture.

It's no surprise that Kasher was planning to use this material in a one-man show. No doubt it would be as attention-grabbing on stage as in print. Fortunately his facility with spoken language extends to his writing: diving and twisting at key moments, injecting levity into melancholy, all the while nurturing a larger point. He speaks of therapy as a "third parent." He knows the power of short, punchy sentences, as when he relates a moment at his father's deathbed, where he offered a speech of atonement: "My affect was frank. My motives were pure. My methods were shit."

Press materials compare the writing to David Sedaris and Augusten Burroughs, and the title invokes J.D. Salinger. Kasher's prose doesn't always live up to those lofty names, but we'll throw in one more for good measure: Kurt Vonnegut. The economy of language, the surreal events smacking against the mundane, the undercurrent of humanity to the horror—it's so deftly rendered that when the book turns serious near the end, the tonal shift feels effortless.

Taken out of context, some lines even have the sublime tang of a Richard Brautigan poem: "Poverty shrank in the face of the anal cat dance," or, "I'd never been raped and murdered, and it seemed totally unpleasant." Considered as a whole, they should inspire jealousy and awe in most comics and writers, not just for having so many compelling experiences to relate, but for having fucking lived through them at all.

San Francisco contemporary Louis Katz has called Kasher "kind of gay and ghetto," and Kasher's self-aware trashiness pervades some of the book's best moments. You feel naughty and a bit thrilled, but ultimately sympathetic. You're granted genuine insight into Kasher's personality, at once fantastically self-destructive and relatable in its instability. Any half-witted biographer would have an easy time of spinning these tales into a ripping good yarn. In Kasher's hands, they become a monstrous, thrilling tapestry of darkness and redemption—one that hangs quite nicely next to his current day job.

March 29, 2012

Rick Shapiro
Unfiltered
Paradisiac Publishing

By Nick A. Zaino III

Watching Rick Shapiro perform, it eventually becomes clear that the man doesn't need to blink like normal human beings. He doesn't recite material as much as explode (see 1998 album *Unconditional Love* or March's *Catalyst for Change*), as if he's been waiting all night or all week or all of his life to tell you this, and he won't be able to rest until he gets it out. Everyone else has been asleep, and it is his duty to wake them up; to tell them what the government is doing, what their culture is doing, what they're doing to themselves. Sometimes it's funny, and sometimes it's frightening. Shapiro could easily step into the world of spoken word and poetry slams, which is, in part, how *Unfiltered* came to be published. Over the course of five years his manager salvaged the bits of paper, napkins and ephemera on which Shapiro had written ideas that never made it to the stage. Some of that material found its way to audiences through a weekly Los Angeles show, *Rick Shapiro: Spoken Word(s)*, and more of his thoughts were adapted by editor Robert Leach for his fiction and poetry journal *Stanley the Whale*.

Much of that material is collected in *Unfiltered*, a book of free-verse poetry, blog posts, e-mails and ramblings straight from Shapiro's spleen. One look at the table of contents ensures that a strange and intense experience awaits: the opening poem is called "Shut the Door on Hope,"

and begins, "I rose out of the shit / Into a pile of stupid shit."
A few other titles include "Angry Stripper," "The Fuck You
Magician," "Atheists and trannies," "The Vagina: It became
America's Heartland" and "Angels piss me off."

As wild as Shapiro can sometimes seem onstage, he
outdoes himself in *Unfiltered*. His poetry and posts are pure
stream of consciousness, unprocessed and unrefined. The
comedy is what he lets out when people are around; this is
what's going through his mind the rest of the time. Thoughts
end abruptly, words are frequently misspelled or placed in all
caps. Polishing that too much would have missed the point.
These are his words directly from his psyche to the paper,
full of tangents, with the amusing bumping up against the
deadly serious. In "Sooo Human," he implores readers to
escape the banal and feel something. "Do something you are
interested in," he writes. "Then do something you're not
interested in, like get married."

Certain themes leave off in one poem and pick up
elsewhere. Shapiro references child abuse in "Shut the Door
on Hope," writing, "They said I looked like Blackie / Child
abused like you've never seen, Man." Later, in all-caps poem
"Can't Love," he admonishes, "OPEN UP RICK, TALK
ABOUT THE BUTTERFLIES THAT COME OUT OF
THE MOTHS OF CHILD ABUSE." Then again in "The
Visit," a story about Shapiro's father confronting him over
allegations of abuse, he discusses surviving welfare and
prostitution, as well as the nature of soullessness.

In a photo of a poem, he writes, "the country will die
cause the ones with the balls were shot walkin down the
street while they said they have great dreams n while they
tried to end all wars." Later again, in a play on the
lifelessness of social media and reality-show culture titled

60

"THEY'RE IN YOUR FACE!" he admits, "I'm hoping to get shot. / That's how I fukking play / This ain't on the internet / It's in your hearts!" He is not impressed with stand up, either, condemning in "Paycheck," "Nobody has balls as comedians and they just want to get in, get in, get in!" Something is trying to coalesce through the din, and Shapiro's approach is to let everything out and sort through it later.

Is any of it funny? Yes, in unexpected places. In "I am Comedy Noir," Shapiro tosses out the strange little nugget "You ever fuck three 18 year olds at once, and get thrown out by the boss that was a midget because you took her mask off…" as if it were just a universal observation. Meanwhile, in "Choose," he imagines a pig auditioning at Julliard to be food at an "upscale sandwich café."

Even when the poetry seems impenetrable, the writing shares that same sense of urgency that makes Shapiro a compelling comedian. *Unfiltered* is not a casual investment for the reader, and definitely not for Shapiro. It can be frustrating, random and then suddenly pointed. Absorbing it can be work. But the message is ultimately liberating. A couple of quotes best sum it up: from "Rick Shapiro the Opera!" "Enjoy yourself and your passions. Kick ass with all of who you are," and again from "Sooo Human," "You are only and always human. / Human! / I love that word! / So human."

April 5, 2012

Jim Gaffigan
Mr. Universe
Self-Released

By John Wenzel

There's always something a little insulting about the qualifications, implied or stated, that follow around Jim Gaffigan's work. Praise of his schlub-with-a-heart material tends to be coupled with semi-apologies for how unchallenging it is. How can someone be this clean and funny and *still* have come from the same artistic tradition as Lenny Bruce and George Carlin? It boggles the mind...provided you're an idiot.

Along with Brian Regan and a handful of others, Gaffigan has been able to pull off a type of humor that's rarely practiced these days, and the general consensus is that his success is all the more impressive for it. Of course, the no-profanity, no-politics school of family-friendly belly laughs recalls Bill Cosby and Bob Newhart more than Bruce or Carlin, but Gaffigan probably isn't poring over his copy of Cosby's *Those of You With or Without Children, You'll Understand* before hitting stage.

Or is he? Gaffigan begins his latest special, *Mr. Universe*, with a bit about becoming a new father (for the fourth time). The toll it's taken on him has apparently turned him from a *muy guapo* Puerto Rican stallion to the pasty, balding lump seen on stage. It's classic Gaffigan: self-effacing, gently desperate and vocally massaged in all the right places. But Gaffigan's appeal isn't just his quirky delivery or lack of F-bombs. It's also his ability to trick out seemingly mundane subjects with deeply sarcastic details, and his knack for inhabiting a bewildering array of characters with a voice that essentially has two settings. If stand-up comedy is all about voice, literally and figuratively, then Gaffigan is also showing how to use it to its fullest. That much is clear from his relatively calm stage presence. Other than a few well-timed head turns and hand motions, his body language is almost nonexistent.

For some comics, that strips away the need for a filmed special, but Gaffigan's command of incredulous expressions, which typically involve a furrowed brow and "Are you serious?" glare, usually enhance the material. Taped in February at Washington D.C.'s Warner Theatre, *Mr. Universe* is being sold for $5 direct from Gaffigan's website. Call it the Louis C.K. model if you want, although with Aziz Ansari selling his latest, *Dangerously Delicious*, in the same way and for the same price, it's quickly becoming everyone's model. (Incidentally, *Delicious* was also taped at the Warner). The time of DRM-free, digitally distributed specials has clearly come, and nothing can withstand their force, provided the comedian has a big enough audience and no need for the usual marketing machinery.

Ironically, Gaffigan feels as prone to censorship as much as any dirty comic, but it's the corporate kind. He spends a good deal of time railing against brand names—in the case of *Mr. Universe*, McDonald's, Dominos and Subway—but since he's not using profanity, it's much trickier to block out the "offensive" passages because the names are deeply woven into the material. This, according to a recent Gaffigan interview with *TechCrunch*, is another reason why he's selling this special on his own.

So is it worth the $5? It is if you've liked anything Gaffigan has done before. *Mr. Universe* is Gaffigan at his most conversational, although it's hard to fathom how this man has eked out so many new jokes from the same small patch of soil. If you've heard a dozen or so punchlines about his pasty looks, put-upon fatherhood, food guilt, or love/hatred of sea creatures, you've heard them all, right? Nope. Gaffigan has a seemingly endless supply, and they work because he manages to locate strange new dimensions to his First-World suffering, even while pointing out how lazy and entitled Americans are. When he talks about Disney World, he doesn't just bitch about the crowds and high prices. He adds a thick smear of absurdity that threatens to turn irredeemably bleak: "At Disney it's like a desperation. You see it on the faces of parents. They're like, 'Uhhhhh, this was an enormous mistake. I hope you're having fun. It was either this or send you to college.'"

A lot of his material is, at heart, a plain-language critique of consumerism swaddled in funny voices, but it succeeds because it's sympathetic. He hates the fact that we take pictures of our dessert at restaurants then tweet about it, but he probably does it himself. "It's all McDonald's," he says, referring to Western junk culture—right after enumerating on the many pleasures of McDonald's fries.

The special's title comes from a joke about freakish body builders, but it might as well be *Mr. Universal.* Despite the stray reference to drugs or porn, Gaffigan has proven once again that a clearly articulated idea doesn't need to be controversial to be powerful.

April 10, 2012

Bridgetown Comedy Festival
Multiple venues, Portland
April 12-15, 2012

By John Wenzel

The Bridgetown Comedy Festival has been likened in *Wired* magazine to a "summer camp for comedians," but also "a victim of its own success" in a *Portland Mercury* article—as if holding a bursting-at-the-seams comedy festival is a bad thing.

Well, it can be. But more on that in a minute.

Bridgetown is about the art of the show, whether it's stand up, a multimedia panel or a character-based set, and there's no perfect-fit metaphor for something that spreads 200-plus funny people across 11 venues for the better part of a week. Especially when the headliners are mid-level names known to nerds and late-night TV watchers, including Janeane Garofalo, Todd Barry, Maria Bamford, Tim Heidecker, Jon Glaser and Doug Benson. It's consciously angled toward the young and hip, which makes Portland, Oregon a perfect home for it.

Founded by Portland comic Andy Wood (now based in L.A.) and co-run with Matt Braunger, Kimberly Brady and others, the festival is also by and for comics. From the venue choices to scheduling and freebies like Sizzle Pie pizza and Voodoo Doughnuts, Bridgetown promotes a general camaraderie. That was clear in the chatter among performers in green rooms and at after-parties at this year's fifth annual event. Whether it was a comic's first year or third, getting a coveted spot there was intensely validating.

The festival's apathy toward media and its seemingly stoned volunteers, however, lent it a loose vibe that one would stereotypically associate with Portland, and made some of the proceedings less than efficient. But that can be forgiven when the density of talent is so impressive—even if it requires short cab rides or frenzied bouts of power-walking to catch overlapping sets.

A mid-evening "*Primetime*" set at Bar of the Gods on Thursday was an early indicator of the diversity and promise: Portland hero Ian Karmel played along with Bryan Cook, Adam Newman, Jaqi Furback, Ben Roy, Robert Dean and others. For a smoky, drafty backroom on Hawthorne Boulevard, it was surprisingly cozy. Karmel fared best while delving into his Italian-Jewish heritage and extolling the virtues of monkeys riding dogs while dressed like cowboys. Roy went full force on the small audience, climbing furniture and lying on peoples' laps as he ranted gleefully.

Ron Funches, another local hero, helped kick off a later set at the Bagdad Theater, which featured Adam Cayton-Holland, Alex Koll, Nate Bargatze and headliner Howard Kremer, among others. Different vibe, same buffet-like approach. In fact, Thursday night in general provided a window into how the same bits did (or didn't) work in various contexts, since attendees were bound to see the same performers do the same sets more than once. An example was loose-limbed madman Eric André, who recently announced an *Adult Swim* series, barely tweaking his locked-in material from the Denver-based *Grawlix* show on Saturday to one across the hall at the Mt. Tabor Theater. The energy worked everywhere. That contrasted with sets from James Adomian,

66

whose mastery of impressions and penchant for slipping into them at a moment's notice made it impossible to see the same set twice.

One could witness Janeane Garofalo do stand up—as she did at Jon Glaser's packed, late-starting *Delocated* showcase on Saturday night at the Bagdad Theater—or talk about movies as part of the Comedy Film Nerds summer preview/podcast at Mt. Tabor with Graham Elwood, Chris Mancini and (eventually) Doug Benson. That show was necessarily general-audience, taking on everything from *Dark Shadows* and *Prometheus* to *The Expendables 2*, but it at least felt like enough of a Comic Con panel to justify the title. One could also see the inimitable Maria Bamford do a straight stand-up set (if that's possible) or see her channel the disturbing life coach Barb in the *Persona!* show, which also featured Upright Citizens Brigade co-founder Matt Besser and others inhabiting various oversized characters.

Like a lot of comedy, highlights came from unexpected places. Adomian playing the Sheriff of Nottingham at *The Grawlix* could have been merely funny, but he stalked the audience with a glass of red wine, maniacally demanding to know where they were hiding Robin Hood. His brilliant commitment to the bit made it one of the undisputed high points. A panel for the forthcoming book and research project *The Humor Code* was one of the most talked-about of the fest, even at 4 p.m. on Saturday. Colorado professor Peter McGraw and writer Joel Warner invited comics Pete Holmes, Myq Kaplan and Mary Mack to sit on the panel, which took a scientific approach to understanding humor and was moderated by *Jordan, Jesse, Go!* podcast co-host Jordan Morris. The comics' banter frequently threatened to overtake their quieter, more hesitant guests (especially Mack's irritating, petulant presence) but there was genuine insight in the Venn diagrams and experiment descriptions. Attendees could also see smaller names like Dwayne Perkins and Jamie Lee—two of the fest's most pleasant surprises—kill it at the Hawthorne Theatre, or watch fest co-organizer Braunger get rapturous applause at his triumphant Saturday night show.

In other words, you could act like you were at a festival: getting drunk and exploring some of the best stand up in America through a bewildering variety of shows that tested even the most hardcore comedy nerds' stamina.

April 17, 2012

Lisa Lampanelli
Equal Opportunity Offender: The Best of Lisa Lampanelli
Warner Brothers

By John Wenzel

If you're only familiar with Lisa Lampanelli from watching her survive the onslaught of idiocy on season five of *The Celebrity Apprentice*, you're the target market for *Equal Opportunity Offender*. And isn't it convenient how the timing has worked out, with Lampanelli remaining as one of the last five contestants and this newbie-oriented compilation available just now, near the end of the competition?

      Equal Opportunity comes on the heels of last year's *Tough Love*, the insult comic's fourth proper album, and offers 14 tracks of the same affectionately racist, homophobic sentiment upon which Lampanelli has built her career. But it's still a greatest-hits release, and therefore immune to the usual live album considerations. Does it work as a cohesive, hour-plus set? Was the crowd into it? Does it sound like it was recorded in a grain silo? All moot. Greatest-hits albums are problematic, and not just for casual fans. Now that we can sample and buy individual tracks online, what's the point of listening to a compilation someone else has chosen for us? Furthermore, you might enjoy the pacing and rhythm within distinct bits, but you never get a sense of where comics are at in their careers. Sure, traditional live albums are edited to sound like a single set, but they at least present the illusion of a seamless, lengthy performance. Maybe the redeeming quality of a greatest-hits collection is that if the bits hang together well enough—whether through thematic cohesion or sheer force of personality—you've got your Desert Island Masterpiece for that artist.

If you already own the stuff from which this Frankenstein's monster was assembled, the good news it that most of it is worth revisiting. The album's title nods not only to Lampanelli's justifications for her humor, but the entire tradition of insult comedy itself, from Don Rickles to Neil Hamburger. And as bawdy as Lampanelli can be with her words, *Equal Opportunity* is about as traditional as it gets. It opens with "The Fag Whisperer," a broad (and broadly written) overview of her Kathy Griffin-like appeal among gay male audiences, including such potshots as, "Thank you, homos, for skipping a night of watching Bravo TV!" and "This big queen right here, he is so gay he jerks off to *Antiques Roadshow*." Not exactly Andy Kaufman. On the similarly-flavored "Homos Are My Favorite People," from her 2009 HBO special *Long Live the Queen*, Lampanelli runs down her "new list of gay terminologies," including such alliterated gems as "Gerbil Jouster" and "Purple Pickle Porthole Pirate." She cracks herself up a few times during the recitation and follows with disjointed jabs at blacks that culminate in a *Blazing Saddles*-derived punchline: "Niggers smell much worse than farts."

The juvenile simplicity and knock-knock joke intimacy is contrasted with the topical, occasionally political humor that has made her a favorite on *The Howard Stern Show*, though both share the same puns, pop-culture references and obsession with sex. "Men Are Good And Women Are Beautiful" offers a view into Lampanelli's mid-2000s club material, when she had to try a bit harder to win over crowds—though, let's be honest, not *that* hard given the lowest-common-denominator subject matter. Lampanelli singles out black, Hispanic, gay and gender stereotypes with the zeal and precision of a young fighter pilot, and thanks to her constant crowd work, she's always got fresh targets.

While no stand up can really be performed in a vacuum, it's still hard to imagine Lampanelli having much to talk about outside of her audience. On later-career material you can hear how she's trained them to respond the way her on-stage persona might respond, garnering groans of disbelief at one point for saying she met "a Hispanic man with a job and no kids... I have located the unicorn!" or having one part of the crowd cheer unselfconsciously when referred to as the "whites only" section.

The problem with insult comedy is that the "What will she say next?" thrill tends to fade after the 100th racial epithet or profanity, and few things other than unfailing cleverness (as with Joan Rivers) or generalized ridiculousness (as with Andrew Dice Clay) can preserve the entertainment value. Fortunately *Equal Opportunity* benefits from its chronological puddle-jumping as well as its track selection, loading up on some longer, more narrative bits near the end to defer the fatigue and allow Lampanelli to wade a bit further into her subjects. The nearly eight-minute "Stereotypes" ping-pongs so quickly between deflating and trading in them that anyone with a preconceived notion of Lampanelli's intentions is left wondering if it's all in fun, or does she really mean it in some deep part of her psyche? Is she a relic of our unenlightened past or the harbinger of our sleazy, hateful future?

Either way: The Queen of Mean is dead. Long live the Queen!

April 18, 2012

Paul F. Tompkins
Laboring Under Delusions
Comedy Central

By Patrick Bromley

Paul F. Tompkins's stand-up act isn't quite the same as Paul F. Tompkins's stand-up specials. His act is a traditional—if absurd—collection of observations and routines, like any stand up, but filtered through Tompkins's unique and particular comic voice. His stand-up specials, on the other hand – in particular 1998 HBO special *Driven to Drink* and now *Laboring Under Delusions*, his new hour-long effort for Comedy Central, have as much in common with monologue-driven one-man shows as they do with traditional stand up. They're more focused and conceptual—more *Stop Making Sense* than regular Talking Heads concert, by point of comparison.

The hook of *Laboring Under Delusions* is that it's all about the bad jobs Tompkins has held (Get it? *Laboring*!), from a retail gig at the cleverly-named Hats in the Belfry ("It must be *really* fun to work there…") to a miserable run at a video store (during which he takes up the new hobby of stealing) to his current job as one of the best standups in the country. The special even takes a short detour to tell some stories about Tompkins's brief acting stint opposite Daniel Day-Lewis in *There Will Be Blood* ("I had heard he was a little bit intense, but he's not…he's really THE MOST intense person that has ever lived.") and the time he repeatedly yelled at Weird Al Yankovic during the filming of VH1's late, lamented *Best Week Ever*.

Those unfamiliar with Tompkins's comedy (for shame, by the way) would do well to indoctrinate themselves with *Laboring Under Delusions*, as it offers some of the comic's most accessible material since his days riffing on pop culture as a talking head on basic cable. After spending years honing a style that combines the silly and the cerebral in equal measure, Tompkins downshifts somewhat to emphasize universality over specificity; everyone, after all, has had jobs that he or she hated, and Tompkins knows just how to highlight that frustration with hilarious bewilderment. While his typical approach to comedy finds him as an absurd voice commenting on the rational world, in *Laboring Under Delusions* he's the voice of reason in an absurd world. Throughout his life, the special suggests, he has encountered an endless series of people whose behavior defies the social contract, from the aforementioned hat-store customers to an audience at a stand-up show throwing ice cubes on stage.

At times, it's Tompkins himself violating the social contract, such as when years of boredom behind the counter lead him to begin stealing VHS tapes from the video store where he worked. What makes it such a distinctly Paul F. Tompkins routine are the little touches; he's maybe the only comic working today who would describe his behavior in those days as that of a "gentleman bandit." Few comedians are as good with the literate turn of a phrase as Tompkins. Only Patton Oswalt and Greg Proops are in his league.

Some of the biggest laughs in the special come not from scripted jokes or one-liners, but just from Tompkins's reactions to things. It's funny when he recalls how, while working at Hats in the Belfry, more than one customer requested to try on the "king hat," but it's even funnier when he deadpans in total disbelief "It's not called a king hat. It's called a crown…What are you doing?" It's the "What are you doing?" that sells the whole bit, as it's indicative of Tompkins's distrust of all humanity, a distrust that comes from years spent working in retail. He's relatable in his incredulity—everyone has felt the way he felt at some point on the job—but at the same time he stands just outside of the mainstream so as to better comment upon it. He is, like so many of the best comics, an observer and reporter of the Ridiculous.

There's a risk that a special like *Laboring Under Delusions*—one with a single specific theme—could come off as gimmicky or limited in scope, but Tompkins is a talented and seasoned enough comic to avoid the pitfalls that could have otherwise sank what he's able to pull off. He knows how to stretch the premise of the special so he is able to present material that may seem tangential (like the Weird Al and Daniel Day-Lewis stories) but clever enough to make sure that everything still fits under the general label of "bad work stories." More than anything, though, it presents Tompkins as a gifted storyteller, and that's not something he's necessarily been known for in the past. There is a confidence and a fluidity to the special that can only come from the years of experience that Tompkins has acquired, and while *Laboring Under Delusions* may not feature the best material he's ever done, he's never been better as a performer.

April 20, 2012

Marty Allen
Palace Station
Saturday, April 21, 2012

By Josh Bell

Marty Allen is 90 years old. That trumps pretty much anything a nearly six-decades-younger reviewer could say about his recent performance at Palace Station in Las Vegas. How many current comedians will still be alive, let alone working regularly, at age 90? Allen is a legend who's been performing stand up since the 1940s, appeared on *The Ed Sullivan Show* alongside The Beatles, was a panelist on *Hollywood Squares* more than 100 times and has guest-starring credits on shows ranging from *Love, American Style* to *The Super Mario Bros. Super Show*. Before Allen and his wife Karon Kate Blackwell took the stage at Palace Station, a screen played a slideshow featuring highlights from Allen's career. There he was with longtime comedy partner Steve Rossi, Jerry Lewis, Ringo Starr, Richard Burton, Ernest Borgnine and many more (including a recent photo with resident Palace Station headliner Louie Anderson).

And then there he was onstage, after about 15 minutes of Blackwell's gaudy musical performance, emerging in a tuxedo (because that's how things used to be done) and launching right into his vintage one-liners, delivering them with precision and verve despite his age and the fact that there were only about 20 people in the audience. Although Las Vegas is famously full of senior citizens, and the show began at 4 in the afternoon, Allen and Blackwell only managed to rustle up a handful of patrons, barely filling the first couple of rows of tables. Blackwell seemed to know half of them personally, greeting them by name during her opening set, and the vibe was more community senior center than Vegas showroom, despite the professionalism of the performance.

For his part, Allen doled out a series of finely honed jokes, jumping quickly from one to the next. Although many were likely decades old, he kept things fresh with references to recent pop-culture figures including Brad Pitt, Jennifer Lopez and Shrek. "I was just named winner of the Louie Anderson lookalike contest," was Allen's opening line, proving he could still craft jokes tailored to his current circumstances. Sure, every joke ostensibly about current events referenced something that happened "today" and probably never happened at all, and the one Obama mention could easily be traded out for any current president, but Allen never seemed like he didn't have a handle on what was going on. He even managed a timely joke about the recent Secret Service prostitution scandal.

The show's main concession to Allen's age was breaking his performance into segments; after 10 minutes of rapid-fire jokes, Blackwell returned to the stage to play straight woman for Allen's routine as a drunken wine-taster, a bit that dates all the way back to *The Ed Sullivan Show* and is in its own way as rote as "Who's on First?" Still, Allen managed to mix things up, either playing up his drunken character or slightly confused about the order of the jokes, and Blackwell dutifully cracked up every time he switched a line around. It was such a comfortable back-and-forth that at one point an audience member shouted out the next line, and

Allen immediately had a comeback: "When did this become a community?"

Broken up by Blackwell's stints singing cheesy oldies to canned background music (including a truly horrific Beatles medley), Allen did another back-and-forth routine as a sex therapist and a whole run of jokes about senior citizens, who are clearly the backbone of his dwindling audience. The sex-therapist routine is another old chestnut (although not nearly as old as the wine-taster), and Allen once again seemed to lose his way a few times, although every time the jokes got out of order, he gave the audience a wink.

Since the average age of the patrons was probably close to Allen's own, the old-age jokes were especially apropos, and much appreciated. They covered the requisite topics ("I was the Grand Marshal for the Prostate Day parade," went a typical line), but Allen gave them an extra zing thanks to his closeness to the material, and to the audience. How many people tour the country speaking to the concerns of septuagenarians and octogenarians in a humorous way, from direct personal experience? Allen is in a class of his own on that one.

Allen connected with each person in the audience, and through it all, he never seemed like he was just going through the motions, delivering every line with a twinkle in his eye. He closed the show by dancing ("after hip surgery") to Blackwell's rendition of "Boogie and Beethoven," looking like he'd be happy to go on for another 90 years.

April 23, 2012

Patton Oswalt
Finest Hour
Comedy Central

By Austin L. Ray

"Anger eventually cancels out comedy," Patton Oswalt told me in 2009. "I think what you have to do is find the thing that delights you, and if you really push [that], then the people that piss you off, it just makes them angry... If you're onstage, and instead of cursing what you hate, you're celebrating the alternative and making that seem better, that's what drives your enemies bugfuck. That's what just drives them into the red."

Throughout *Finest Hour*, his latest Comedy Central special (out on DVD today), Oswalt celebrates all manner of things. ABBA, the "torture porn of the Old Testament," his child's dancing, Bob Seger, *Green Lantern* comic books, a guy who "plays [a puke bag] like Dizzy Gillespie," even the simple pleasures of a food court filled with courteous people or having drinks and seeing a movie with a sibling. (Many of the more tangible items that make appearances in his jokes throughout are even featured in a wildly silly and impressively thorough bonus-material montage, "Stuff Patton Mentions.") Even the way he walks out onto Seattle's Moore Theatre stage and mouths "Oh my God," at the packed, rapturous audience points to a certain type of celebration: an exuberant sense of appreciating just how far his hard work has gotten him in the past two and a half decades. You'd be psyched, too, if you got to stand in front of a couple thousand folks and turn a scenario in which a supermarket denizen says, "I want all the ham!" into a rich and ridiculous time-traveling-warrior epic.

More than simple celebration and appreciation, *Finest Hour* depicts Oswalt as a man learning as he goes. He still talks plenty of shit on people taking their beliefs to illogical ends or the passive-aggressive, nonsensical hatred of homosexuals, but he also turns the focus on himself. Whether it's a quick apology for being a dick in the past to people who wore sweatpants in public ("They're a miracle," the new father admits), his "jock-rocking" all the boring stuff that happens in his life (from going to the post office to masturbating to internet porn when "he should be teaching his daughter to read"), the depressing banality of Weight Watchers meetings or mispronouncing the word "brewery," his self-mockery knows no bounds. Oswalt cycles through several scenarios—from slaphappy rhyming songs to fart sounds—that both illustrate what a goof he is and eradicate any wall there might have been between performer and audience.

"What I love about Patton is his precision," Paul F. Tompkins told me for that same 2009 story. "He writes these beautiful, rich, textured pieces that have so much happening in them conceptually and have such exact language." Based on that criteria alone, this special very well may indeed be Oswalt's *Finest Hour* yet. Phrases like "an unbroken belt of stink" and "Dr. Seuss on an angry pussy hunt" manage to be thoughtful, illustrative and laugh-out-loud funny at once. Elsewhere, "neck-deep in the crazy pool" and "chainsaw-titted clown" work that same magic. Illustrating Tompkins's point, these are words that sound great together, grab the listener's attention and somehow walk the line between hyper-intelligent highbrow and make-your-mother-blush lowbrow in such a way that they stand up to scrutiny, even out of context.

"I might as well put on Blackface," Oswalt says at one point of auditioning for a role as the gay best friend in a romantic comedy, later spinning it to point out a weird, condescending trend in mainstream movies. "I wanna be the first dumb, gay best friend in the history of cinema," as opposed to the "quip machine" that so many stereotypical Hollywood roles portray. Elsewhere, he discusses how we have gotten rid of slavery, but we still have the circus. Even when jokes like these hinge on him eventually turning to dicks or defecation, there's an underlying thread that Oswalt is working to make the world a better place. He's learning and striving just like everyone else, and he doesn't always have the right answers. On *Finest Hour* he acknowledges his wavering atheism, wondering if maybe he should believe in 8,000 gods instead of none, and admits that maybe he's a little more into Ambien than a dad in his 40s should be. It's refreshing to hear a successful, outspoken dude saying, "Hey, maybe I don't have any idea what's going on either." After all, what's the point if we all keep getting older and don't learn a damn thing?

"I hope and expect to look back on everything I think and feel right now and say, 'Wow, I sure got a lot wiser,'" Oswalt told me toward the end of our 2009 conversation. "I hope—I really hope—for that. I still feel wisdom and humility are just specks on my horizon, though."

April 24, 2012

Todd Glass
Laughing Skull Lounge
Thursday, April 26, 2012

By Austin L. Ray

"I have a very hard time saying that," Todd Glass told Marc
Maron on a January episode of *WTF*. After coming out as
gay on the podcast, Maron had suggested that maybe Glass
should own the words, but he was having a little trouble.
"Don't get this wrong. I don't want anyone to be ashamed of
who they are, especially younger people. I always hated using
that term, and that's partly why I've always been
sympathetic to people who don't [want to be labeled]. I hate
that word. But I like it better than the other word:
homosexual."

Glass, who came out more than a decade ago to his
parents and has had a steady partner of 15 years, added that
many people already knew he was gay, but it was
nevertheless incredibly difficult to say in such a public forum.
Presumably a great weight has been lifted off the 47-year-old
comedian's shoulders, but old habits die hard, and for a guy
who's joked about his "girlfriend" on previous albums, it's
perhaps unsurprising that he stuck to the status quo
Thursday night at Atlanta's Laughing Skull Lounge. Glass's
sexuality is his own, and given that he had trouble even
saying the words during the podcast on which he chose to
say them, it's understandable if he's not yet ready to
incorporate his now-public preferences into his act. But it's
also a little weird for those in the know. Like when he

smelled a female audience member and joked about looking down her shirt, for instance.

"I know how to do the dramatic thing; keep 'em waiting," he announced—perhaps in a coy reference to the recent *WTF* podcast—immediately upon taking the stage to Roger Miller's "Walkin' in the Sunshine," the first of several songs played throughout the evening. He then announced that the show was over, thanked the audience for coming to the Laughing Skull, and closed the curtains. He came back, of course, and performed a self-described "choppy" set of manic arguments and explanations, both with himself and others, for a little over an hour. It will be interesting to see how much of this material ultimately ends up on the special he has coming out in the fall, as well as what form it will take when he tours soon with Louis C.K. (Both items were announced by the evening's emcee before Glass took the stage.)

Despite his admission to the contrary, Glass put on a solid show, not to mention worked the audience thoroughly. I.e., he spent *a lot* of time on crowd work. Some of it was amusing (making a guy uncomfortable about the Zima he didn't buy), some of it charmingly awkward (when he called a girl out for her cell-phone usage, then let it go because she was embarrassed, which he approved of), and some of it was a singular, tell-your-friends experience. (He made *another* cell-phone user call her mom, and then proceeded to converse with her on speakerphone for the room's delight, the ridiculously earnest/sweet mom, Connie, both asking, "Are you for real?" and saying, "I'm sorry, I don't talk to strangers.")

Even in the less-rewarding moments, the dude worked, and he worked hard. Glass's set comprised a multimedia element of at least four pre-planned songs that played into bits, crowd interactions including pitting the audience against itself, choosing his sides alternately and seemingly on whims, and even traditionally cheeseball, easy punchline jokes ("Do I look like Fred Flintstone and Mel Gibson's baby?") that he'd rattle off at random before spinning the microphone like a rock star. (He'd also drop it to the ground throughout the night, a fine effect that eventually grew old, but never predictable.) This tireless ethic was best epitomized by a two-minute ShamWow bit, originally a 30-second joke based on the fact that it's just a rag that soaks up messes. As the story goes, David Cross once challenged Glass to extend the gag to four times its original length, offering him $2000 to do it. Glass couldn't pass up the opportunity, because at the time he needed the money. The final product was equal parts exhausting and deliriously giddy.

"I cannot listen to stories about kids killing themselves any longer without thinking, 'When are you going to have a little blood on your shirt for not being honest about who you are?'" Glass asked himself on the *WTF* episode in question. "I can't do this any longer." Although his material hasn't changed much since the announcement, there's a sense that he feels true relief. He ended with Sammy Davis, Jr.'s "I've Gotta Be Me," mouthing the words and waving his arms around, marching from side to side of the stage as everyone walked out of the room, smiling and feeling great about themselves.

April 30, 2012

Kyle Kinane
Death of the Party (Vinyl Reissue)
Stand Up! Records

By Austin L. Ray

Of the 10 tracks on Kyle Kinane's uproarious debut album, *Death of the Party*, originally released in 2012 on ASpecialThing Records (Paul F. Tompkins, Jen Kirkman, Doug Benson) and receiving the vinyl-reissue treatment today on Stand Up! Records (Hannibal Buress, Marc Maron, Dylan Brody), only one of them is less than five minutes long. In particular, the epic "I Know What I Want"—an extended meditation on, amongst other things, Bob Seger's "Night Moves," moving to Los Angeles from the Midwest, how people relate to each other via food and crashing a Ford Focus—clocks in at close to 10 and a half. To say that Kinane is a bit of a storytelling comedian is an understatement. But like any great story, from one told on the spot over drinks between close friends to a well-worn and increasingly embellished tale told by an old-timer trying to impress his grandkids, it takes some work (or at the very least an inborn knack for this kind of thing) to make it truly pop.

Kinane possesses that, and it's fitting that Stand Up! would give this record a limited-edition vinyl pressing. Arguably the best comedy release of 2010—and serving as an introduction to one of stand up's brightest (and rising) stars, a man that has since found himself busy with touring, voiceover work and a Comedy Central special, amongst other things—this record is a modern-day classic. It's the kind of thing that makes sense to own on vinyl, a format that caters to tangibility. Sometimes you only want to repeatedly listen to a track or two off a release. Other times, if you like an album enough, you want to own the CD. But with the truly greats, the actual best of the best, it just feels right to own a 12″ piece of wax that you'll handle cautiously as you put it on, hopefully in a comfortable place in your residence, in which you'll then kick back with a beverage to enjoy the content.

"I can only describe this fella as looking frustrated from having run out of flesh to tattoo," Kinane says on one of the finest tracks here. The bit is based on a bowel movement, but, as he claims, it's actually "about the triumph of the human spirit." Over the course of six minutes he details an emergency bathroom visit involving a too-small stall in a Latino-gangster bar in Chicago, the gentleman described above and a surprisingly happy ending. Like much of Kinane's material, especially the stuff that he's written since *Death of the Party*'s original release, the guy telling the story is the butt of the joke, and life really ain't that bad when you take a step back from it to consider the bigger picture.

As previously described by *The Spit Take*, "Kinane earned a creative-writing degree in 2002 from Chicago's Columbia College. He's no dummy. Perhaps best described as Schlubby Dude Chic, all ample beard and hoodies, comfortable sneakers and jeans, and a voice akin to the excitable rasp of *It's Always Sunny in Philadelphia*'s Charlie Kelly (albeit in a lower register), his style may suggest otherwise. Yet these are also Everyman traits that make him one of the most likable dudes in stand up. He's like the Dubya of comedy with one important caveat: you want to have a beer with him, but he's not a war-mongering fool." His most notable characteristics—street-smart wise-assing, an actual book-learned education and bar-regular conversational deftness—mix together like a classic, artisanal cocktail, resulting in the kind of material that rewards repeated listens. And if his recent shows are any indication, he's only sharpening that material, taking it to smarter, sometimes-thematic new heights.

And that's going to be the fun part, the going forward. Kinane's only tightening up his wizardly wordcraft, albeit to the point where such phrases as "stripped-bare toothless cog spinning freely and ineffectually in the working machine of society" deftly and hilariously roll off his tongue as if they're second nature. Although he likes to play up the slob angle on Twitter, and indeed, some of his best material involves pizza, beer and the like, it's Kinane's storytelling prowess that's carrying him, and it's only becoming more rewarding with time. Or, to hear him tell it in a recent interview, as long as there are conversations to be had, there will be good times ahead: "I'm a bar-room bullshitter type. I don't write out my conversations first. I go and sit there and bullshit with people and have a laugh, and that's how I try to approach comedy. I'm going to go up there and hang out with everyone–let's all laugh at something together." A pretty reassuring thing, when you think about it.

May 1, 2012

The Apple Sisters
1943
Self-Released

By Steve Heisler

There's a saying in comedy that's so old, I don't even feel the need to put quotation marks around it: If you try to be everything to everyone, you'll wind up being nothing to nobody. True comedy is born from minutiae, and now more than ever—given the niche audiences that can be garnered from podcasts and self-produced live shows—it's a liability for comics *not* to play to their finer points, however limiting that may seem.

The Apple Sisters are a core (Nailed it!) example of finding abundant success in specifics. Rebekka Johnson, Kimmy Gatewood and Sarah Lowe parody a 1940s-era radio program at their live shows and on their Earwolf-distributed podcast. They make wisecracks about FDR and World War II, create fictional commercials for bygone products and treat domestic abuse as a matter-of-fact inevitability. Their bits are evocative of a time long gone, delivered with over-the-top bravado that manages to stay charming. In their "Corndy" sketch, a commercial for candy corn, the women eat corn off the cob and spit out the kernels in the rhythm of a typewriter—all while managing to rock sweet three-part harmonies. If that's not commitment, I don't know what is.

On *1943*, the Sisters take the finer points of their act to a whole new level of finer-pointing. Their focus is on a particular year of the 1940s, and the group nails the target with bull's-eye accuracy. Right from the start, the object of each song's joke is crystal clear, from the bamboozling nature of ads to Las Vegas's façade of allure. But the Sisters have a plan; *1943* is so polished it feels almost calculated…until you stumble onto one of its many expertly placed surprises.

Limiting themselves to a single year opens up unexpected avenues for satire and silliness. To highlight a woman's obsession with staying thin, the Sisters sing about a great new weight-loss product: a tapeworm. They even give it a name, "Tippity Tappity Tapeworm," and have it speak in a shrill, ear-piercing voice between musical refrains. Not only are they singing in exaggerated, old-timey-radio style about tapeworms, but there's humor coming from the sheer joy of hearing this tapeworm goad the girls into eating way more than they're comfortable with. At another point on the album, Paul F. Tompkins pretends to be FDR addressing the nation, going out of his way to alleviate any fears that he might be wheelchair-bound. He mentions running and walking all the time, then apropos of nothing exclaims, "Jazz splits! I just did a bunch of them…with my *working* legs!" The Sisters let *1943*'s perception of FDR guide this silly-yet-simple bit, and its memorability is proof enough they should always follow their instincts.

The Apple Sisters have a hell of an ear for music, and thus are able to embed jokes in the notes themselves. "Man Song" is purposely sung in a low key (a "manly key"); the notes naturally get higher as the song rounds the bend, but rather than switch back to their beautiful womanly voices, the Sisters remain committed to the bit and strain to hit high notes in their man-voices. The song "Killer Daddy" starts as a creepy lounge number co-starring a sleazy guy cooing promises of stardom (played by a dead ringer for Danny

DeVito), but ends as an uplifting almost-gospel song, the titular daddy overwhelmed and slightly turned off by the Sisters' enthusiasm. Then there's "War Is Great!," where they seamlessly combine timely American ditties like "Home on the Range" and "Grand Ole Flag" into a medley that collapses into a cacophony of misplaced lyrics. They begin by singing about patriotism but end more confused than ever about what the word even means.

Every piece of *1943* is hand crafted and meticulously planned. No part of the album makes the act feel anything like a gimmick. There are tracks that indicate the end of "Side A" and "Side B," but even those have jokes that build; on "Side A" the Sisters literally just take 10 seconds to tell you to flip over the record; on B they pray you start the album over and wonder if the recorder's still running as they casually bicker. Plus there are jokes that take the entire album to pay off. "Ring! Ring! Ring!," the second track, is one of the catchiest songs out there, let alone in just the comedysphere: The girls try to impress a movie producer (Tompkins again) with an off-the-cuff pitch involving telephone operators, cats and a murder. The third-to-last track, "Three Merry Murderers," may include a cat or two.

Jokes hit on so many different rhythms, and the songs are rife with sweet harmonies and infectious choruses. *1943* is a blueprint of how to make a great comedy album: Know exactly what you want to say, and push yourself not to deviate.

May 8, 2012

90

Lizz Winstead
Lizz Free or Die: Essays
Riverhead Books

By Nick A. Zaino III

Lizz Free or Die: Essays isn't a memoir, but it is memoir-ish. And it's not a traditional book of essays, a series of self-contained pieces with a definite thesis. But the writing does not lack for opinions. Lizz Winstead takes a more dialectical approach, walking the reader through her life in roughly chronological order via a series of interconnected pieces she calls "messays."

Winstead starts with her childhood, when her political ideas began to form. She wondered about the origins of the bronzed hands folded in prayer hanging on the wall of her family's home and resisted the notion that she was on the standard path to marriage and kids. She didn't like real babies, so receiving a plastic one with which to play house didn't interest her, a predisposition that made her somewhat of a tiny pariah. She also was disappointed to find out the Church wouldn't allow her to be a priest, and that when she did well on a high-school psychology test, her teacher told her she'd make a good mother instead of a good psychologist.

The independence and contrarian streak of a stand-up comedian were present early, and Winstead gives herself a lot of credit for these virtues. When she's admitting her lack of patience for other people's points of view (the part of her personality she calls "Lizzilla"), it feels like a compliment. It's as if she were asked that clichéd old job interview question, what she thinks her greatest weakness is; her answer that she can't stand stupidity.

"All Knocked Up," a turning point early in the book, sees Winstead dealing with teenage pregnancy. This is where she especially sticks to her promise to avoid a lurid kind of tell-all. In that moment of her life, every institution on which Winstead was raised to rely betrays her. The narrative is not about how the physical situation resolved, but how the incident shaped her philosophy, ending with a mutual rejection that sets the scene for her to develop her nascent comic point of view.

Those looking for some comedy history will appreciate the story of how Winstead came up through a robust Minneapolis scene. Twin Cities music in the Eighties is much chronicled, and Winstead was in the enviable position of seeing Prince perform early sets and forming friendships with members of Hüsker Dü, Soul Asylum and the Jayhawks. One of the funnier stories involves Winstead emceeing an air-guitar contest at a local club, and the resulting inadvertent exposure.

In her chapter on creating *The Daily Show,* Winstead is full of wonder at landing her dream job—a show she believed would allow her to be a part of the solution to the growing problem of media imbecility—on her first try. One of the main criticisms leveled at the earliest version of *The Daily Show* was that its humor depended on meanness, ambushing the clueless with cameras and making fun of easy targets. It was Winstead's job to discern between the truly incisive and the just plain mean, something she describes as part of her learning curve. She glosses over her departure, writing that she left "for complicated reasons that are far less important than my wonderful experience of creating and bringing it to life."

She is not quite as reserved about her time with the Air America radio network and on the atrocious MTV show *Burned*. Winstead and her old *Daily Show* partner Brian Unger were hired to produce *Burned*, a reality show wherein unsuspecting young men on spring break were baited into revealing their inner assholishness for the cameras. Winstead and Unger had no other job options, and protested the network's decisions at just about every step. That's the excuse given, but it's not an easy sell.

In contrast, Winstead is unabashedly proud of Air America. She believes the network evoked some positive change and did some good work, but that the whole venture was doomed due to the cluelessness of different ownership groups. "I helped develop a network that bore some pretty awesome fruit," she writes, calling Rachel Maddow "one of the purest voices in cable news," and Al Franken "one of the purest voices in the United States Senate."

There are a couple of attempts at formula: each messay ends with a quick summation of what Winstead learned from her experiences, and in places she provides definition for words made up to illustrate a point. Most of the lessons are about learning to trust instincts, and Winstead found her best blueprint in her penultimate essay, "Dielarity." It's a beautiful and heart-wrenching story of her family gathering at her father's deathbed. The humor is dark but loving, with a wonderful payoff (thanks to her father's sense of humor). Winstead shows a deft touch in capturing compelling details, a fitting final growth spurt to cap the collection.

May 10, 2012

Reggie Watts
A Live at Central Park
Comedy Central

By Austin L. Ray

Reggie Watts isn't exactly a comic. He's a funny man, yes. A
funny, distinctive-looking man who does ridiculous and
sometimes hilarious things on stage, sure, but he's not a
comic. He's a musician, too. Not a musician who strums an
acoustic guitar and tells bad jokes over simple chords like
many a hack. He took piano and violin lessons for 11 years,
creates complicated loops, beatboxes; he possesses actual
musical knowledge. He is difficult to describe because A)
what he does is so unlike what anyone else does, and B) you
kinda start to sound like a fanboy even if you don't like the
material. It's that awe-inspiring.

It makes sense, then, that his Comedy Central special
isn't exactly a comedy special, either. *A Live at Central Park*
begins with idyllic harp strums and our hero zapping a
would-be purse thief in the titular park with a *Street Fighter*-
esque *hadouken.* The special proper starts just after that, with
Watts addressing the New York crowd and easing into some
standard material. Throughout *A Live*, the action cuts to a
sketch where Reginald (played by Watts) hangs with a lady
friend on a blanket in the park, waking from a dream and
trying to make sense of a world that may or may not be
playing a giant trick on him. But more on that in a minute.

If you're familiar with Watts's work, chances are you
found it one of three ways: his internet videos like "Fuck Shit

Stack," his opening for Conan O'Brien on his Legally Prohibited From Being Funny on Television tour, or the music he created for Louis C.K.'s FX show, *Louie*. Note how varied those three things are, add the fact that his performances—including this one—are almost always 100 percent improvised, and you start to get an idea of what a singular talent Watts is.

"Wow, that guy's crazy," he says of Woody Harrelson toward the beginning of *A Live*, though he's clearly referencing Woody Allen. "I'm glad I'm not that guy." Much of the special's first 10 minutes or so consists of Watts pacing the stage and saying whatever comes into his brain. He thanks the people who made the performance possible, but it quickly gets absurd, leading to the inventors of AstroTurf and the stool holding his effects pedals. He ultimately raves about AT&T (who never drops calls) and JetBlue for whatever reason.

Eventually he starts segueing into music, the responding laughter only slightly less awkward during the non-funny parts than it was during the proper spoken-word pieces. That's the thing about Watts: He rarely breaks character or even smiles during the quote-unquote punchline, and the effect it has on the audience is an uneasy "Well, maybe *that* was the joke?" If you're in on it, reveling in the discomfort of others only makes the spectacle more rewarding. If you're not, as a few people in the crowd definitely weren't, well, maybe it's not quite as fun. At any rate, it's mostly music from there on out, Watts crafting gems like this off the top of his head over loops, beatboxing and keyboards: "Don't worry, people. If we fuck up too bad as a human race, nature's just gonna kill us all. It's all right, it just sucks for us—not for the earth, yeah. It's been around for billions of years; we don't even matter to it."

Elsewhere he discusses how guns are louder than knives, plays a crab-cake gag on the crowd (long story), does "a song about sex" that unfortunately becomes unlistenable due to Comedy Central's censoring, and hilariously covers Radiohead with his own send-up of "Idioteque." It really is a grab bag, but in the best sense. The final song begins with Watts riffing on Zippos versus cell phones, masturbating in front of a computer, hawks/eagles/bluejays and social networking before he sings, impressively, "Falling in love isn't the same as fallin' out of love," hanging on the notes, fading out to beatboxing.

The special ends with the sketch, which has developed between bits. Reginald wakes from a dream, finds a flyer advertising himself (as Reggie) playing Central Park and is thrust into a great quest—involving hobos, the Cool Castle, park rangers, a tiny television and a squirrel named Parsons, amidst many other odd details—to find out the truth. Turns out he's the founder of Corncubes International, a conclusion that makes about as much sense as any, really. "What a crazy dream within a dream," the lady friend says, and Reginald, who is now back to Reggie, makes a face until someone off-camera calls "Cut!" Watts then shakes his head and exclaims "Jesus Christ," because he knows how special and awesome and ridiculous and fantastic and bizarre it is that he gets to do this stuff for a living.

May 11, 2012

Tenacious D
Rize of the Fenix
Columbia Records

By Michael Tedder

Considering the amount of time (five-plus years of development), effort (innumerable smoke sessions) and money they poured into it (you can see where the $20 million went), mock-rock duo Tenacious D probably hoped their feature film debut *Tenacious D in The Pick of Destiny* would be a big hit. But from listening to *Rize of the Fenix*, it's hard to shake the sense they're secretly happy it was a huge flop, because it gives them a great setup to work with.

Just as their 2001 debut album was an outlandish parody of Hookers 'n' Satan rock excess from two dumpy-looking guys who spent their lives mistaken for roadies until "Tribute" became a viral hit (before viral hits were really even a thing), *Fenix* is a parody of the "comeback" album bands make after burning out creatively, flaming out commercially, breaking up, hitting rehab and then telling *Behind the Music* their new album is their "best work ever."

Part of their debut's joke was that these guys didn't look like conventional rock stars, but they sang about cock-pushing groupies so sincerely you occasionally forgot they were really two well-regarded comedic actors. Here, the meta-textual joke is that The D have no real need to come back, but couldn't resist a ripe target. *Pick's* flop didn't halt Jack Black's steady stream of movies or keep Kyle Gass from doing whatever it is he does in his spare time. If anything, this endeavor is probably viewed by Black's agent as time that could be spent on *Kung Fu Panda 3*.

Their extra-musical success and Wikipedian love of rock clichés gives The D a perspective and luxury the Mötley Crües and Styxs of the world don't have when making their actual please-just-love-us-again turns. They delight in both mocking their failure ("When *The Pick of Destiny* was released it was a bomb / And all the critics said that The D was done") and skewering every part of the *Behind the Music* template, from creative overreach ("Flutes & Trombones" is a send-up of the arena-rock impulse to prove artistic bonafides by using an orchestra on every damn song) to interpersonal strife (In "The Ballad of Hollywood Jack and the Rage Kage," Jables "Climbed the ladder of stardom before him / He watched as his indie credentials flew right out the door / He'd make millions and then he'd go out and he'd make even more millions / He'd screened KG's calls and snorted coke off the ass of a whore.")

Like the best mimics, Tenacious D love the source material they're satirizing, and they get the details right on *Fenix*, from the prime-era Metallica whiplash drums (courtesy of D superfan Dave Grohl) on "They Fucked Our Asses" to the Iron Maiden gallop of "Deth Starr" and the almost too-accurate Survivor homage "To Be the Best," though the constant Eaglesian faux-classical guitar gets old after a while, thematically appropriate as it may be. Call 'em a joke band, but their hook-writing chops and Black's Angus Young bellow is legit. If Tenacious D hadn't pitched themselves as a parody act, it's doubtful they would have still broken through to the Olympic levels they survey, but longhairs who spend too much time at Guitar Center would have loved them just the same.

For the record, *Tenacious D in The Pick of Destiny* isn't all that bad of a film if you go in with the proper expectations. Or, you know, high. There's kind of plot to it, but it gets dropped fairly quickly so the dudes can get into whatever hijinks they talked New Line into funding that day, from the classic (Grohl as the Devil) to bits that probably sounded good at the time (uneven, misshapen comedies are not a crime, but wasting an Amy Poehler cameo is.) It's a mess, but an enjoyable enough one if you're on their wavelength. Same goes for the return to form. If The D had focused on the triumphant-rebirth thing a bit more, this could have been on the level of their dorm-room classic debut, but too many songs go nowhere (they seem to have either forgotten to write a joke for "Throw Down" or simply thought the idea of Gass fighting was so inherently hilarious that their workday was done) or revisit old ground to diminishing returns ("Senorita" is no "Fuck Her Gently"). Let us not even speak of the catalog of scatological terms that is the hidden track.

The D's best songs find humor by zeroing in on the pretensions and lusts that fuel and destroy rock gods, and then making those the focus of their art rather than the ruin of it. That they found prime material by exploring the supposed wreckage of their career seems appropriate. And if the final result falls well short of the glorious comeback it's supposed to be parodying, that's probably appropriate as well.

May 15, 2012

Hannibal Buress
Animal Furnace
Comedy Central

By Austin L. Ray

When I last interviewed Hannibal Buress, I asked him about the seemingly nonsensical title of his forthcoming release, *Animal Furnace*, and he told me it was something "goofy and dumb" that someone had sent him on Twitter. Clearly I hadn't yet said the two words out loud, especially following his name, which brings the goofy dumbness into focus. Or maybe it's just a silly rhyme and nothing more.

This subtle, weirdly clever slow burn is a lot like Buress's comedy, which frequently garners comparisons to the late Mitch Hedberg. "I'm doing a little work here," he tells the security guard at the doorway of NYC's Gramercy Theatre in *Animal Furnace*'s opening bit, and you know that's how he really said it. While Buress gets worked up during his act, often raising his voice, it's usually to make a point. His default is more of a relaxed, patient flow, his words coming out at a nice pace, carrying you along, hitting you with laughs when you might not expect them. For example: "When you put a garbage can on your head, it limits your peripheral vision about 100 percent," he says early on. The bit goes on to repeat the words "garbage can" every third phrase or so, and the results are a mesmerizing avalanche of giggles.

Animal Furnace's material is delightfully varied and absurd. He touches on his *Saturday Night Live* experiences (including the sketch he wrote for Megan Fox where she killed people with musical scatting—it didn't make it to television), taking down Homeland Security about the liquids rule (with talk of Snickers and "bomb juice," no less), shaking hands with Jimmy Carter and the many dangers inherent in that, lovely and unpredictable stories about lack of sex and excessive vomiting and well-timed farts, how "urban" doesn't mean "black," the Holy Ghost dancing in Arby's and so much more. As a group, these may sound kind of ridiculous, but it's Buress's sense of silliness and confidence that ties them all together.

Many of Buress's jokes have a personal/social moral at the end, from "You shouldn't hang out with this person," and "Do I kill myself or do you kill yourself?" to "You should expand your social circle," and, unsurprisingly, there's an obvious absurdist quality in that as well. It's almost as if he's a comedic guidance counselor, pointing his audience to better decisions. But at the same time, he'll be the first to admit it's all kind of bullshit. He's just in it for the laughs, as he should be.

Fans of Buress's Jeezy joke from a couple years back will be happy to know that he's expanding his rap-humor repertoire. Of Odd Future's lyrics "Kill people, burn shit, fuck school," he jokes, "Doesn't it seem like they're getting more reasonable as they go along?" following up with the fact that they're really just a half step or so away from saying they hate spam or hotel-television channels or updating iTunes. Elsewhere, he talks about how rap has ruined the ways he talks to people, including his mom, to whom, after telling him she needn't be paid to watch her grandkids, Buress concludes, "Yo, mom, money over *everything*."

102

Not many comedians working today can consistently deliver laughs in such a clever and refreshing fashion. He's got this uncanny knack for simultaneous swagger and self-conscious hilarity; he's as happy to tell someone else how to live their life as he is to tell a story about messaging a woman on Facebook before realizing she's in high school. He's flat-out laugh-out-loud throughout; *Animal Furnace* is almost embarrassingly consistent, a mix of big hilarity with subtler moments woven in between to break up the rhythm just so.

Now that Buress is no longer writing for *30 Rock*, and given the quality presented here, one has to hope he'll focus on comedy full time. Or at least fuller time. He's got myriad TV projects cropping up, from his co-hosting duties on *The Eric André Show* to the Fox pilot he's working on with Jonah Hill. Hopefully those projects—and his recurring role as a hobo on *30 Rock*—will pay the bills and allow him to keep doing stand up until it's taking care of the rent. Luckily, he's not content with his relative fame. Toward the end of our recent conversation, when I mentioned that things were really coming around for him, what with the shows and opening for Aziz Ansari, he cut me off. "Yeah, but you just said 'opening,' though," he interjected with a laugh. "That's great, and it's helped me build my audience, but I want to be, you know, headlining those venues, and that won't be for another couple years. There's a lot more work to do."

May 18, 2012

Gary Gulman
No Can Defend
Comedy Central Records

By Daniel Berkowitz

On his second album, *No Can Defend*, Gary Gulman responds to the audience's opening applause with, "I think I... I think I absorbed it." The tendency, as he explains, is to "deflect" the praise, but he cannot, as "It's just the way I was raised." He then segues into one of his few bits about being Jewish: "Cautious, are we cautious. Oh, my Lord. And we have every right to be; we've been in a couple of pickles over the years."

It's in decisions like this where Gulman's savvy comes to light. He's not a *Jewish comedian* as much as he's a comedian who happens to be Jewish. And thankfully and appropriately, he does not mine this tired backdrop for 45 minutes; rarely even does he self-deprecate as a direct result of his heritage. Aside from comparing his visage to that of the Fruit Loops spokesbird, Gulman never takes the easy route. Instead of enlisting as a permanent disciple in the overcrowded cult of Woody Allen, Gulman acts as simply a tourist. By not relying on his neuroses or an ostensible persona as vehicles for continuous cheap laughs, Gulman is able to instead borrow what makes those paradigms workable, add to them in ways that amplify their utility, and not pigeonhole himself as any one kind of comedian.

On a superficial level, Gulman's in the mold of a Jerry Seinfeld: an observational comedian who is able to adeptly extract humor from seemingly mundane subjects.

But while Seinfeld constantly pushes the listener away by rarely talking about himself, Gulman occasionally brings the listener in, showing how what he observes can bring him grief.

A perfect example comes on "The @ Sign." Speaking to how the sign has become pointless shorthand for "at," Gulman laments, "We're shortening two-letter words now?" And on "Ode to Netflix, Part 1," he castigates Blockbuster for a slew of misdeeds, not least of which is their "criminally loose definition of 'New Releases.'" "Why is this a new release?" Gulman asks. "Because it's in color!?"

In instances like these, Gulman only shows off half his range, as he's capable of turning both inward for self-analysis, as well as outward for cultural commentary. And in rare moments of beautiful artistry, he's able to expertly conflate the two.

"I can get movies instantly on Netflix, but that's a burden, too," Gulman proclaims. "I don't know if you can tell, but I gotta get out of here and watch movies… I'm gonna die with 100 movies in my queue." This sentiment, though perhaps immaterial to some, depicts a mind struggling. Struggling with…something.

It's a stretch to say Gulman is making an implicit comment on modern-American society's lust for overindulgence. What his remarks do convey is the notion that anxiety comes in all shapes and sizes. There are bound to be listeners who feel that sense of urgency because of their ever-expanding Netflix queues, listeners who, in some form or another, feel a similar sense of anxiety over comparably frivolous things, and listeners who get where Gulman's coming from. For them, Gulman's comedy—like any good comedy—hits home and reassures them that, yeah, there are other fucked-up people out there, too.

In this way, what separates Gulman from equally funny comedians is his genuineness. There's a quality about Gulman that makes the listener feel at ease. There are no attacks, there's no aggression waiting to pop out, there aren't any tricks—there's just consistent, down-to-earth comedy. Gulman is eminently relatable: His placid demeanor is warm and inviting, and although he's not a Louis C.K., openly listing all the shitty things he thinks and feels, he's nevertheless being honest. We know the low-level anxiety he promulgates comes from a sincere place, and from his tone and delivery we can discern that it is quite real.

In fact, Gulman would do well to turn inward for material more often. Yes, he is primarily an observational comedian, and yes, he is admittedly skilled at what he does, having crafted a style with which he is certainly comfortable and sharp. But his best moments come when he imbues something outside himself with his own sensibility. His eight-minute closer about his ideal sexual roleplay is a prime example. Or when he outlines why he stole a muffin or how he wishes he could go back in time to tell his younger self to take typing classes more seriously. These aren't necessarily moments of observational comedy, but they're not confessions of the soul, either. They straddle the line between the two extremes, and they do so masterfully. And when Gulman toes that line and settles into his perfect little space, the results are both hilarious as well as rewarding.

June 5, 2012

Michael Ian Black and Meghan McCain
America, You Sexy Bitch:
A Love Letter to Freedom
Da Capo Press

By Nick A. Zaino III

The concept behind *America, You Sexy Bitch* is a kind of
forced, political *Breakfast Club*. Take two people who only
know each other through Twitter—a liberal comedian and a
conservative pundit/daughter of a Republican senator—stick
them in close quarters and see what happens. Instead of
Molly Ringwald and Anthony Michael Hall, it's Meghan
McCain and Michael Ian Black. And instead of detention, it's
a month-long road trip in an RV, visiting each other's
families, partying in New Orleans and Las Vegas, firing
guns, seeing Yakov Smirnoff in Branson, interviewing
Dennis Kucinich and talking to everyone they meet along the
way.

      The hope is that these two strangers can end their
trip realizing each of them is a gun-toting Republican, each
of them is a pro-gay rights Democrat, and freeze frame
pumping their fists on the football field. Black even
references the film toward the trip's end, echoing Hall's
doomed question, "We'll still be friends Monday, right?"

      Spoiler Alert: the answer is…yes, apparently. If the
answer were no, would they still have released the book?

      At turns, Black and McCain are both engaging, off-
putting, thoughtful, dogmatic, loose and catty. The book is
told in a "He Said, She Said" format, alternating between each

author's point of view in every chapter. They frequently try to get on each other's nerves: McCain relishes seeing Black get uncomfortable around guns or when someone they don't expect to be turns out conservative. Black knows McCain is sensitive about the perception that she's a spoiled senator's daughter, and he throws it in her face.

Both revel in their respective stereotypes, and each have their respective blind spots. Black wears his linen pants and Crocs everywhere. A Bill Clinton acolyte, he dismisses the man's lying and cheating mainly because he remembers peace and prosperity during Clinton's presidency. McCain loves guns, country music and anything with an American flag on it. She offers Reagan as her president of choice, writing that Reagan never had an affair in office and was never impeached. Neither of them mention Clinton bombing Iraq or Reagan's Iran-Contra affair.

Still, there is a palpable sense that Black and McCain are trying to get along, if only for themselves. And also for America. No, really. Each truly believes in the concept of "America," and though their definitions vary wildly, they both agree it has something to do with inclusiveness. They don't go so far as to preach acceptance, necessarily, usually remaining too philosophically split for that. At one point Black writes that, despite their best intentions, neither has managed to convince the other to change their mind about anything. Their combined plea is more along the lines of "Can't we all just get along?"

And while politics looms over everything, there are apolitical moments. This is supposed to be entertaining affair, after all. So sometimes McCain, Black, Black's assistant Stephie and the group's driver, Cousin John, just get drunk together and have a good time. They try to put everything aside and see if they can get along as people, which is just as much the point they are exploring as any specific ideology. Sometimes it backfires and they wind up bickering, but usually they just drink and laugh.

The two surprise each other along the way, and the people they meet surprise them in turn. Black has always seen the Log Cabin Republicans as a small, ineffectual fringe group; when he meets them, he finds a group of dedicated, professional people and has the epiphany that America is mostly comprised of small, ineffectual fringe groups trying to change things. McCain finds herself rethinking America's drug policies when her hippie researcher hosts in Washington discuss how useful ecstasy has been in treating post-traumatic stress disorder in battle veterans. Both believe in gay rights and global warming.

Ultimately and somewhat predictably, they wind up understanding each other better. Black comes to hate the way McCain is often portrayed in the press. Despite her bravado, he writes, no one is more likely to question her convictions than Meghan McCain herself. And McCain relishes seeing Black enjoy himself on a shooting range. The final irony (again, a Spoiler Alert here) comes when they finally reach Black's home to cap off the trip. At home, Black is the conservative family man with a wife, two kids and (literally, as he points out) white picket fence. McCain is the one who questions the value of marriage and can't see herself settling down. It's a surprising reversal of stereotypes.

The book proves that people can get along if they put politics aside and treat each other as human beings. That's an important message, but the nagging, unwritten postscript is "What happens next?" Yes, everyone is still friends on

Monday, but the political problems remain. Getting along is a baby step that feels much bigger.

June 11, 2012

Jimmy Fallon
Blow Your Pants Off
Warner Brothers

By Josh Bell

Who knew that throughout his years on *Saturday Night Live*, his failed movie career and his underdog talk show, what Jimmy Fallon really wanted was to be Weird Al Yankovic? Fallon's new album, *Blow Your Pants Off*, features non-stop musical parodies, with no sketches or interludes or spoken comedy bits, and it's hard not to compare Fallon to the venerable master of song spoofs. Fallon is less inclined to create straight-up parodies (merely switching out the words to a popular song) than he is to craft mash-ups that creatively combine two incongruous styles, but the Yankovic comparison is hard to ignore, especially on some of the album's weaker efforts.

Most of the songs on *Blow Your Pants Off* were originally performed on *Late Night with Jimmy Fallon*, and many went on to be viral hits online, so fans are likely to be familiar with a great deal of the material even before their first listen. Some very clever songs are showcased, especially Fallon's combinations of his near-flawless impressions of classic-rock stars (Neil Young, Bob Dylan, Jim Morrison) with bits of pop-culture ephemera, but almost all of them are better appreciated by just heading over to YouTube (or one's video-sharing site of choice) and searching for the originally broadcast performance. The parade of celebrity guest stars makes more of an impact when one can see them, and many of the songs were first enhanced with entertaining costumes or dance moves that can't be experienced in the audio-only versions.

The worst example of this is closing track "Let Us Play With Your Look," the theme song to a recurring *Late Night* segment. It's literally impossible to understand what's funny about this song without seeing the accompanying visuals; otherwise it's just Fallon singing the title line over and over again. The audience is laughing, but there's absolutely no indication of what they're laughing at. At the other end of the spectrum, Fallon's impressions sometimes come off better when he can't be seen dressed in whatever ridiculous outfit he wore for the performance. It's easier to imagine Neil Young singing the theme song from *The Fresh Prince of Bel-Air* or Jim Morrison crooning children's book titles when all there is to go on is the impeccably re-created voice.

As goofy as those songs are, they also show that Fallon has a real understanding of the essence of certain iconic rock stars, and he can expertly parody their images with simple juxtaposition. Dedicated progressive activist Young singing the theme of a sitcom that celebrates excess is a perfect—and yet unexpected—send-up of his style and his message, and it has the added bonus of hitting nostalgia sweet spots for two different generations of viewers/listeners. The album's other Young parody (featuring a guest appearance from the real Bruce Springsteen) finds Young singing Willow Smith's "Whip My Hair," and if one doesn't listen too closely to the lyrics, it almost sounds like it could be one of Young's more abstract art-folk songs.

"Butterfly in the sky/I can go twice as high" sounds *exactly* like a line from a Doors song, but it's actually the opening couplet of the *Reading Rainbow* theme, another effective, unlikely combination of material and performer. Fallon generates humor from simply listing the titles of children's books in the voice of Doors frontman Jim Morrison, and *Late Night* house band The Roots reliably mimics The Doors' musical style. The Roots are the album's not-so-secret weapon, exhibiting remarkable versatility on songs like the Justin Timberlake-assisted "History of Rap" and *Late Night* staple "Slow Jam the News," here represented by an edition guest-starring Brian Williams (sadly, the recent President Obama "Slow Jam" appearance didn't make the cut).

As musically accomplished as those songs are, though, they're not nearly as fun to listen to as they are to watch. One of the greatest strengths of Fallon's show is the sense that everyone involved is having tons of fun, even when what they're doing is sort of dopey. Fallon audibly cracks up a few times during the songs on *Blow Your Pants Off*, but the interactions that drive him there aren't visually apparent. The rendition of Rebecca Black's "Friday" featuring Stephen Colbert and Taylor Hicks was a joyously silly moment on *Late Night*, but on record it's just a mildly appealing rendition of a lame pop song.

The numbers not culled from Fallon's show are even less impressive, and they compare the most unfavorably to the Yankovic oeuvre. Tracks like "New French Girlfriend," "Cougar Huntin'" and "You Spit When You Talk" are built around obvious, weak jokes, and would have barely been filler-worthy for Yankovic. Fallon is great at creating an atmosphere of exuberant camaraderie celebrating the fun of ridiculous pop culture, and that feeling comes through on the album's best moments. But make no mistake: he's got nothing on Weird Al.

June 12, 2012

Ernie Kovacs
Percy Dovetonsils...thpeaks
Omnivore Recordings

By Austin L. Ray

Ernie Kovacs was a prolific, tax-evading, mustachioed entertainer of the highest order, influencing many future titans of comedy with his work in the Forties, Fifties and early Sixties, from David Letterman to Chevy Chase and *Saturday Night Live* to Jimmy Kimmel. He got his start as a Trenton, NJ radio DJ in 1941 and eventually worked his way up to national television, where he would make and spread his name through myriad programs and characters, the most popular of the latter arguably being the star of this previously unreleased studio album that found itself shelved for more than 40 years. But more on that in a minute. As for the comedian, though his *The Ernie Kovacs Show* was nominated four times, he would tragically meet his end in a 1962 car wreck just before he was posthumously awarded his first—and only—Emmy (for that of Outstanding Electronic Camera Work).

Percy Dovetonsils, meanwhile, was a lisping, probably-if-not-definitely gay, absurdist fictional character created by Kovacs while working at Philadelphia's WPTZ studios in the early Fifties. Clad in gag glasses with eyeballs drawn on them—allegedly purchased for a dime by a Kovacs associate on a hunt for comedy props—and sporting curly, greased hair and an outrageous, zebra-print smoking jacket accented with a lavender scarf, Dovetonsils would be

115

offensive—indeed, is still kinda offensive—by today's more tolerant standards. But listening to the innocent silliness of his material and the confidence of the character, it's not an impossible stretch to understand the context or even outright dismiss the faux pas of the past, much like an elderly person using the term "colored." The times, they are a-changing, after all, and comedy remains one of the foremost tools of accurate cultural reflection.

Over gentle piano composed and performed by Kovacs archivist Ben Model and based on Kovacs audio that dictated how much music should play between each cut, Percy reads outsizedly absurd poems with such self-explanatory-and-thoroughly-ridiculous titles as "Some Pertinent Thoughts of Julius Caesar While He was Being Assassinated," "Ode to Stanley's Pussycat" and "The Night Before Christmas on New York's Fashionable East Side." The poems themselves range in length from 17 seconds to just over four minutes. Sometimes the humor derives from the lack of content, while at other times the gag stretches far longer than it should, the building tension a deliberately small but relentless joke in and of itself. For his part, Percy laughs at his own cheesy jokes (one of many humanizing aspects of his doofus persona) and, perhaps out of false modesty, occasionally chortles at the mere mention of own name. He's a Character in the capital-C sense, and his shtick is laid on in a predictably heavy-handed fashion.

Perhaps unsurprisingly, *thpeaks* serves its purpose less as a hilarious, long-playing album that will inspire frequent listens and more as a collectible relic of comedy history. (The first 1000 vinyl copies of the Omnivore Recordings release were even pressed on lavender vinyl.) Its very presence is a tribute to both Kovacs's unwavering commitment to artistic expression, no matter how ludicrous, and his unquestionable influence, as evidenced by the silly characters who have populated several decades' worth of television programs as well as many a stand-up bit.

Archivist Model dug this collection up after hearing about and having no luck finding it for years, not even through eBay's vast reaches as the internet decidedly become the world's finest source for collectible excavation. As a result, unearthing *thpeaks* sounds like nothing short of discovering the veritable chest of gold at the end of a rainbow. "Dissolve to me, sitting at a table at an archival storage facility in California, in October 2008…" Model writes in the album's liner notes. "The 142-page inventory included some items that, according to my archivist-minded 'spidey sense," appeared to be mislabeled." He eventually stumbled across a few cans of 1/4″ audio tape unmistakably bearing Percy's name, and the rest, as they say, was conversion-to-digital history.

This long-lost album comes barely a year after the exhaustive six-disc/780-minute *Ernie Kovacs Collection* that Shout! Factory released last year on DVD, and right on the heels of April's month-long Kovacs retrospective at Astoria, NY's Museum of the Moving Image. At the latter, comedian Robert Klein spoke of Kovacs's genius, particularly in terms of his ability to pull off ridiculous things (gorilla jazz trios and, um, gorilla ballets, for example) at a time when ridiculous notions weren't exactly the TV norm. Or, as television journalist Jeff Greenfield said at the Astoria retrospective in April, "[Kovacs] led the deconstruction of the medium of TV the way Jon Stewart does today in politics, and really beat it to death." That very image would probably shock Percy Dovetonsils to the core, despite he himself very much comprising a part of Kovacs's subversive DNA still remaining in the modern medium's genes.

June 19, 2012

Jim Norton
Please Be Offended
Epix

By Daniel Berkowitz

As one of the most reliably entertaining and consistently
provocative comedians working today, Jim Norton has
crafted a persona in recent years that is as shameless as it is
singular. And in *Please Be Offended*, his newest hour filmed at
the Ohio Theatre in Cleveland, Norton preserves the
qualities that have made him one of his generation's foremost
comedic voices, while amplifying them in ways that only
enhance his legacy.

Norton's an asshole, a scumbag and a pervert. And
he'll readily assign himself any of those labels. Norton's skill
stems from his confidence: he knows who and what he is. He
knows his style, he knows his cadence, he knows his
audience. He's depraved, but he's not out for shock value.
He's intelligent, but he's not verbose. Like any entertainer
worth his salt, Norton knows his limitations. He's entered
that holy sphere of comedians in which we know what we're
getting with each new hour: while we have only a general
idea of his specific subject matter, we know how he's going to
come at us, and we know he'll split our sides throughout the
process.

Norton has four modes: celebrity attack, self-
deprecation, sexual humor and cultural commentary. While
these four arenas are distinct—Norton will devote entire bits

to each—they are exceedingly capable of being conflated. And to this end, Norton is something of a magician. What is so paradoxically brilliant about Norton's style is that even when he's firing off a legitimate diatribe about something real and controversial, he is quite capable of bringing his primordial, sexual inclinations into the fold. In this way, he softens the blow to those who disagree by giving them something to laugh at. That said, if one doesn't agree with Norton's views, he couldn't possibly care less. A look at his special's title says it all: *Please Be Offended.* In Norton's view, if you're offended by comedy, you have no business listening.

A sound display of Norton's sorcery arises when he discusses the merits of the TSA's airport pat-downs. In the midst of responding to people's continual complaints about invasion of privacy, Norton concedes the situation can be worse for women: "To have your breasts mushed together, and your own breast milk poured down your throat, and your buttocks separated... Whatever else I would do if I had that job." He then mimes a TSA official abusing his power by inserting his fingers into a woman's vagina, whisking away excess liquid, and giving them a creepily extended smell before oozing the confirmation, "You're no terrorist."

The eminently quotable George Carlin said that the comedian's aim is to not only find the line and cross it, but to also make the audience glad that he did. To this end, we'd be disgusted if Norton were simply making crude jokes and gestures for the hell of it. But we know everything is with purpose; everything leads somewhere. Every detour has an ultimate destination. And with Norton—unlike the quintessential Bill Hicks acolyte—the level of comedy is never sacrificed for the sake of making a point.

Toward the end of his bit on invasion of privacy, Norton exclaims: "I would be very interested to hear anybody's alternative solution, but how do you stop the mentality of a guy like the underwear bomber?... He was going to blow himself up, *dick and balls first*. All suicide bombers are repulsive, but *dick and balls first*. Even though it's only a nanosecond, there's still a nanosecond where you're like, 'My dick and balls are gone!'"

By Norton's account, airport security is a necessary evil. What he'd prefer to direct his ire at is the hypocrisy of the American people when it comes to perceived injustices. In Norton's view, we continually "act like civil-liberty victims," yet, in reality, we're nothing but "morbid jizzbuckets who like to watch other people's lives go into the toilet." After all, why didn't anyone who complains about invasion of privacy speak out on behalf of Tiger Woods or Mel Gibson when their personal lives were public fodder?

There's a striking disconnect between these two seemingly disparate ideas. But like a good cultural commentator, Norton is able to elucidate the substance below the surface. And like a good comedian, he's able to do so with biting humor.

In the same breath that Norton mocks Woods and Gibson, he also humanizes them. As a self-avowed pervert, Norton empathizes with the two celebrities and points out our hypocrisy about and unfairness toward them. They're human. They err. They're not perfect and they're not role models. But neither are we. We're all as capable of bad as we are of good. And if that notion offends you, then so be it. Norton wouldn't have it any other way.

June 29, 2012

Matt Braunger
Shovel Fighter
Comedy Central

By Michael Tedder

Matt Braunger got his big break on *MADtv*, and became a
minor Internet comedy celebrity for starring in the absurd
web series *IKEA Heights*. He has a strong sense for measured
storytelling and feeding off the energy of a live audience.
He's especially good at making "Oh, that was no good!" faces.
(His look of utter self-bafflement after nervously asking a
woman "Where do you live?" within seconds of meeting her
is especially memorable.)

Braunger's a respected stand-up comedian, but it's
hard to shake the sense that it's not where his heart truly
lies. Which is not a complaint, necessarily. It's just that there
are many parts of his new special, *Shovel Fighter*, where it
seems he never really quit making sketch comedy after
MADtv was cancelled. He just brought the sensibility to a
different medium.

Shovel Fighter basically breaks down along two lines:
Braunger shares sad-funny moments from his life, often
framing the story so his tales of epic hangovers and working
in soul-sucking day jobs are as pathetic as possible. Though
well-told and lined with memorable details (like him
accidentally saying "Lonely Man Dinners" instead of
"Hungry Man Dinners)," these parts mainly seem like
connective tissues between his more out-there moments.
Because what Braunger truly excels at is creating short, self-

contained vignettes that are rich in visual detail and filled with "Wait, what?" moments that are sometimes *Funny* funny and sometimes *Why is he talking about being forced to murder his best friend with a shovel?* funny.

Braunger often gives the impression he's a frustrated short-film director, or an expert sketch comedian without a sketch show. He thinks and writes like a sketch writer, each interaction with a different character he plays ratcheting things up just a bit more until things are so weird you forget the original premise. There's a strong influence of the *Saturday Night Live* sketches and movies Will Ferrell made with Adam McKay, wherein seemingly normal situations only exist so they can spiral out of control as fast as possible. A bit where Braunger yells "You do not speak!" at someone for daring to talk during the imaginary hangover-only section of an airline is so Ferrellian in its cadence that it almost seems like an intentional hat tip.

Given the option, it's easy to imagine that Braunger would like to make weird little four-minutes movies. Instead he's working with the tools he possesses at the moment: his voices, his microphone and his body. His gingerly skipping, awkward dancing and feigned barfing help create a sense of action and multiple characters. Of course most of the best stand-up comedians are storytellers, but there's a sense of scope that sets Braunger apart. His stories feature multiple characters, action, plot development and compelling visuals…and are often so packed with strange ideas that they barely fit onstage. It won't be a great shock if his participation in an all-clown pub crawl or recounting how the original Bob's Big Boy was a poor child who cleaned floors in exchange for a sack of hamburgers become fodder for animated YouTube hits.

Sometimes these stories serve to amplify society's quizzical codes of conduct, such as an extended tale about how men have no real-world etiquette but deeply ingrained strip-club etiquette. Women have the reverse, and therefore male strippers have it much worse than female strippers. This leads to one of the more memorable getting-hit-in-the-balls jokes in recent memory, though it seems like the bit was originally rooted in a riff on arbitrary gender binaries and male discomfort with female sexuality. That is, before Braunger keeps pushing the idea far beyond reason, eventually landing on something satirizing what men think women find desirable, but mainly seems to exist so he can say the phrase "Let me wash your car with my ropy penis." (It should be noted that Braunger comes off as a genuine feminist, eager to mock those who believe in strict gender norms. Or maybe he just really likes to cook for himself and finds Fleshlights disgusting for non-political reasons.)

Braunger can craft a story illustrating the complexities and incongruities of daily life via his characters' unexpected actions. But sometimes he creates stories just for the sake of being strange and to straight bug out the audience, such as when a riff on a crappy job segues into a story about a warlord forcing him to participate in medieval shovel battles. Braunger provides no indication that he's moving from something that really happened to a weird flight of imagination, and the humor comes not so much from any particularly funny parts than from the way he keeps a straight face without acknowledging the transition.

His knack for slamming his sketch-minded oddness into straightforward comedy storytelling produces a jarring effect that is all his own. Braunger's a child of both stand-up and sketch comedy, beholden to nothing but his own strangeness.

July 13, 2012

Todd Barry
Super Crazy
Comedy Central

By Austin L. Ray

You probably know Todd Barry, even if you don't think you
know Todd Barry. He's worked on a veritable laundry list of
amazing television/movies (*Louie, Flight of the Conchords, The
Wrestler, Bob's Burgers, Bored to Death, Chappelle's Show, Aqua
Teen Hunger Force, Delocated*), all the while crafting his
snarky stand up for audiences all over the world. On the
latter, he's dropped three albums and a *Comedy Central
Presents*, but somehow this is his first hour special for the
humor behemoth.

    Much of *Super Crazy*'s material starts like so: a
simple setup ("I did a show in South Carolina..."), followed
by something a little bit weirder (guy asks him about making
tons of money doing comedy), followed by Barry plucking
the weirdness apart, mocking the absurd person or thing ("I
can tell by the question you're in it for the right reasons."),
often beating that absurdity like so many dead horses. The
slow-burn unraveling is Barry's calling card, and it works
more often than not throughout *Super Crazy*. The best
moments are when he, in character or not, gets befuddled by
how long a bit has stretched out. ("Oh my God, I forgot that
was an answering machine myself," he says during one.)

    Barry's dulcet, breathy deadpan is mesmerizing in its
restraint. Like Steven Wright with extra smirk, Barry's
delivery gets into a warm and fuzzy rhythm that can

alternately help or hurt his jokes, depending on the viewer's expectations and tolerance. Annoyed by a mildly shticky characteristic? Barry will likely drive you batshit, his voice slowly grating away at your sanity. But it's easy to get into his zone if you give right of way to his sarcastic observations.

And boy, are they sarcastic. He thanks a praise-seeking cab driver who picked up Barry instead of a woman—despite the fact that Barry was there first, and that's how cabs are supposed to work—for "passing up a guaranteed opportunity to get laid." Elsewhere, while describing an apartment hunt, he visits a particularly unimpressive listing: "A tile bathroom—I can't even imagine what that's like. I wonder if it's like every bathroom I've ever been in…in my entire life…including the one at the bus station?"

Out of context, these barbs may sound uninteresting, juvenile or lacking in insight, but again, it's all in the delivery, the unraveling. He starts with a simple premise like "Young people use stupid phrases," points to a couple of them, then spirals out from there, referring to community-college students as old Bluesmen, then soliciting fruit suggestions from the audience to further point out the silliness of it all. If it seems kinda random, that's because it is, but the reward is in the delight of seeing where Barry's mind takes a commonplace incident.

His stage persona also lends well to bravado. "This guy's slapping his knee; he's doing everything right," he notices at one point, smugly assured that his comedy is worthy of the man's amusement. "He said 'Of course,' as if there were no choice. And there isn't a choice." Elsewhere he mentions his killing on the open-mic circuit, how he's our time's best topical comedian, and so on. The difference between a cocky, in-your-face comedian and Barry is stark, and it helps add to his likability. The arrogance is a put-on, of course, but it's not aggravating, either.

Paradoxically, self-deprecation is also in the mix. When fans ask Barry if things like a drunkard throwing up in the front row is a setup, or a "30-woman bachelorette party wearing chocolate dick helmets and talking throughout [the] show," only to confront him at the bar after they've been kicked out, he does a good job of making his life seem a lot harder than it probably is. But when he turns it around to telling the joke about puking and an actual person pukes during said joke, and the whole "magical" incident scaring the living shit out of the audience ("His jokes come to life!"), it wraps up the bit with a nice little bow of resolution. Yes, the sarcastic man and the arrogant man and the self-deprecating man are the same man. Barry is large; he contains multitudes.

Super Crazy ends on a positive note…sort of. As the story goes, he's been thinking about the happiest moments in his life. Without spoiling the bit, let's just say it comes at the expense of some asshole he's rolling his eyes at surreptitiously. But would you really have it any other way? Like his role on *Louie*, which exists mostly to mock the show's titular creator, Barry is here to keep the ridiculousness of the world in check. Or at least to allow us all to laugh at it with him. And what's more positive than that?

July 20, 2012

James Adomian
Low Hangin Fruit
Earwolf

By John Wenzel

It's easy to get excited about James Adomian. The Omaha-bred, L.A.-based comedian is a gifted improviser and impressionist, always a joy to watch (and listen to) as he disappears into various characters at the flip of switch. His slot during *The Grawlix* show at this year's Bridgetown Comedy Festival, for example, found him sailing through an extended bit as the Sheriff of Nottingham, prowling the crowd with a glass of red wine while he begged (in his best, most deliciously gay cartoon-villain voice) to surrender Robin Hood or face execution. It was a stunning and utterly hilarious showcase of his talent. He's also been known to slip into bull's-eye impressions of Jesse Ventura, Vincent Price, Sam Elliott and George W. Bush at a moment's notice.

To most people—at least those outside the L.A. scene—Adomian is just a finalist from *Last Comic Standing*, so *Low Hangin Fruit* is meant to exhibit all sides of the man. As such, it feels petty to complain that his straight stand-up material doesn't always gel around his jaw-droppingly accurate impressions. But it's true.

After hearing Adomian do so many characters on various *Comedy Bang Bang* shows, it's almost a shock to hear so much of his "real" stand-up voice, which sounds like a particularly gruff, peppy Paul Rudd. He begins the album with some trifles—an easy but relatable jab at Facebook's ubiquity, some complaints about the inscrutable dialogue on *Game of Thrones*—before cutting into the core material, which finds him draping luxuriant impressions over the skeletal frames of an idea. "Ass for a Face" and "Breathe Until the Spirit Exhales You" are just excuses to hear his excellently schlubby Paul Giamatti and confidently insane Gary Busey, but they're so worth it. The humor exists as much in Adomian's sharp theatricality as the absurd content, even as the jokes unfurl a bit past their logical length. And Adomian is a pro when it comes to relishing the unkempt edges.

Whether he's casting Ron Paul as a Jimmy Stewart-like populist ("He has Viking opinions and *Leave It to Beaver* delivery.") or nailing the pervasive "gay villain" voice (Imagine the Decepticons screaming at each other backstage at a drag show.) his vocal aim is true. He exults in old-timey accents and characters lifted from classic Hollywood movies, but he also channels sports announcers and political buffoons. The range comes in handy when he dives into "Openly Closeted," in which he rattles off a list of outdated (and fake) euphemisms for "gay," his mustache-twirling accent selling it perfectly. He also playfully follows up the question, "Are there any more gays here tonight?" with "Is there anybody here *in* the closet? Thought I'd check."

There aren't many openly-gay male comedians out there, especially compared to the many gay and gay-friendly female comedians, so it's refreshing to hear him take the material head on (so to speak). His descriptions of different types of gay bars should ring particularly true to anyone who's visited a few—especially when invoking the weirdly apologetic names of small-town ones (Rumors, Scandals, etc.). But Adomian never feels like he's pandering or trading in stereotypes, even when he smartly exploits them (see "Football Season" and "Straight Beer Ads").

If this sounds potentially limiting, it's not. At least for people who place more value on humor than politics. The true test is whether or not the observations would be funny on paper, regardless of who they're coming from, and they are. But the wheels tend to loosen when Adomian gets riled up, not because his aim is off but because he occasionally loses himself in the repetition and volume, seemingly under the spell of his own voice. The thrill of experiencing Adomian is that he could go off in any direction at any time, but it doesn't always make for cohesive comedy.

A couple bits feel tacked on, like his "Bushsteps," which serves as a quick excuse for a George W. impression. There's cleverness to spare, but *Low Hangin Fruit* would have benefited from some judicious editing. Still, there's so much old-school showmanship that it feels like a neon-ringed billboard for Adomian's raft of talents: "Come for the impressions! Stay for the seven-minute hidden track about opening for Joan Rivers at a South Florida casino!" And let's not forget the album title, a self-deprecating nod to Adomian's material as well as a goof on his homosexual prowess. It's a rough chuckle that would make any Eighties road dog proud.

Since *Low Hangin Fruit* is a dizzying mash of old and new voices—all coming from the same person—it's no surprise it doesn't always hang together. But when it does, it captures the talent and spark that has lately put Adomian on the lips of so many comedy insiders. (Please get your mind out of the gutter.)

August 13, 2012

Amy Schumer
Mostly Sex Stuff
Comedy Central

By Daniel Berkowitz

Some may find it easy to label Amy Schumer a one-trick pony: As the title of her special suggests, she talks about sex, and she doesn't talk about much else. By virtue of being a woman and rooting her act in the realm of our most primitive emotions and behavior, Schumer is, to some, purely out for shock value. To make such a sweeping assertion, though, is not only an insult to Schumer's remarkable cunning and perception, but it also casts a dark cloud over any comedian who bases his or her act around one pronounced subject.

Filmed at the Fillmore in San Francisco, *Mostly Sex Stuff* is an edited-down 41 minutes about, well, mostly sex stuff. Schumer makes no apologies and she doesn't beat around the bush. Throughout her set, she discusses off-color subjects like waxing her vagina, the horror she experiences upon viewing an uncircumcised penis and her unique method for combatting pregnancy (Hint: for Schumer, it's Plan A). All the while, she leaves her audience in stitches.

Yet it is at this juncture that the essence of Schumer's persona and material comes under scrutiny. The central question is why is the audience laughing? Are they laughing because Schumer is funny, crafting well-written bits with good timing and a nuanced delivery? Or are they laughing because they're shocked into it? Is Schumer, a woman—one who, even today, is not as normally expected (or afforded the chance) to make dick and fart jokes—throwing such subversive, unexpected material at her audience that they are literally shocked into laughter?

A good measuring stick to use upon contemplating this dynamic is whether the audience would laugh if, for example, Louis C.K. were making jokes of this ilk. The answer is undoubtedly yes, all things being equal. Moreover, would the audience laugh if George Carlin were going on an epic rant? Or if Jim Gaffigan were singing the virtues of fast food? Or if Marc Maron were overanalyzing a look a guy gave him? All these comedians have (had) a niche. So the question changes; has Schumer found her happy zone, wherein she can tease out humor with her own personal slant, or does she use jokes about anal sex in the same way an unpolished comedian might use the word "fuck" as a crutch? One's answer is probably indicative of the openness of his or her worldview.

In this way, for one to speak ill of Schumer's narrow focus is pretty tantamount to sexism. After all, it seems that every female comedian with a dirty mouth comes under fire sooner or later—Joan Rivers, Sarah Silverman and Whitney Cummings instantly come to mind. This is a common complaint against female comedians, yet most students of comedy can call bullshit on this fallacy fairly quickly.

This is not to say, however, that Schumer is immune to criticism. Too often she reels off throwaway lines that, while certainly funny, are not even remotely close to the quality of her longer jokes. "Once you go black," Schumer advises mid-bit, "your parents don't talk to you anymore." Jokes like these are cute and surely worthy of laughter, but they exist in their own little vacuum with no real substance behind them. These lines come off on occasion as unnecessary or contrived, whereas her more natural, organic material is so free-flowing and expertly delivered that it casts these lesser jokes in a comparatively inferior light as a result. Schumer would do well to pare down some of these asides and steer away from feeling compelled to use them to chop up and punctuate her bits. Her material is so strong, and her voice so worthy of attention, that all they do is detract from an otherwise exceptional performance.

This criticism aside, *Mostly Sex Stuff* is, by any stretch, an accomplishment. What separates Schumer from many comedians (male and female) is that she, without question, puts herself on the line. Every dirty word and foul thought she espouses can be traced back to her singular mind—a testament to her willingness to spill her guts. Schumer is more than comfortable humiliating herself for our pleasure. This is not without purpose, though; Schumer's not talking about her vagina for the hell of it. It's on her mind, she deems it worthy of discussion, and if she can do so with biting humor, then that's good enough.

Coupled with her 2011 album, *Cutting*, *Mostly Sex Stuff* undoubtedly proves one thing: Schumer has balls. And hers are as big as any male comedian's out there. What more could a comedy fan ask for?

August 16, 2012

Sleepwalk With Me
Directed by Mike Birbiglia
IFC Films

By Nick A. Zaino III

Mike Birbiglia fans will come to *Sleepwalk With Me* already
familiar with the material, enough that at times they will be
able to guess exactly what is coming next. Birbiglia has
covered this ground in his stand up, as a storyteller, in print
and as a one-man show. *Sleepwalk* is almost his brand. Which
begs the question, is there anything new for Birbiglia to
explore here?

Fortunately for Birbiglia and his audience, the
answer is yes. Through each iteration and each retelling,
Birbiglia has refined the story, and *Sleepwalk With Me* the
film is the most pointed and succinct version yet.

There are three main threads: Birbiglia, or rather his
stand-in Matt Pandamiglio, is at the tipping point. He has
been with his girlfriend Abby for eight years, he's trying to
make it as a comedian, and his sleeping disorder is getting
worse. He seems unwilling or unable to move forward, but
the tension builds as each problem complicates the others.

The dimension the film adds is watching Matt/Mike
struggle while he has to interact with other people. It
emphasizes his awkwardness and shows how his actions have
a real effect on others in a way that a monologue can't. When
Matt brings up not wanting to get married early on in the
film, Abby (played by Lauren Ambrose) deflates completely.
His father (James Rebhorn) is always berating him for not

making plans as his mother (Carol Kane) meekly tries to defuse the tension. And in one important moment, the audience can actually see him bleed.

The first trace of hope comes after a revelation on a road gig. Matt bombs with an audience doing material about Cookie Monster and panda bears. He opens up about his personal life to the headliner Marc Mulheren (played with a sleazy charm by Marc Maron), who tells him to put that stuff in the act. From then on, his comedy career picks up while his relationship with Abby deteriorates, which in turn pushed his sleepwalking to a more dangerous level. The scene in which Matt finally caves to the pressure with Abby is both heartbreaking and hysterical. And then, of course, there is the final turning point and epiphany at the La Quinta Inn. The photos from the real-life incident over the credits are a nice touch, too.

Stand-up fans should especially enjoy seeing Matt's transformation from open micer to a road comic making a living. Birbiglia doesn't exaggerate the arc—he's not playing arenas at the end, he hasn't had a TV break, and he's not any sort of national sensation. His breakthrough figuring out who he was as a comic was more important, and thus a bit of who he was as a person. There is clearly still plenty of hard work ahead, driven home by the insane triptychs that illustrate his travel plans from gig to gig. There are also a lot of comics playing minor roles; in addition to Maron, Hannibal Buress, Jessi Klein, Kristen Schaal, Henry Phillips, Wyatt Cenac and David Wain all make cameos. Eugene Mirman can also be seen bringing Matt offstage in what looks like Union Hall in New York, home to Mirman's *Pretty Good Friends.*

It's impressive that this is Birbiglia's directorial debut. The fact that he's worked so hard on this material seems to have allowed him to storyboard more effectively, to know where each beat should be, even if the medium is completely new to him. He had help in the form of co-director Seth Barrish, who directed both of Birbiglia's one-man shows, *Sleepwalk* and *My Girlfriend's Boyfriend*, for the stage. Barrish is also credited with the screenplay, along with Birbiglia and his brother Joe, as well as *This American Life* host and producer Ira Glass, who also produced the film.

Glass's influence is detected in the pacing of the film. It has the feel of a *TAL* story, most obviously because Birbiglia has told the stories there. There are also similarities to work by other comedians-turned-filmmakers Louis C.K. and Woody Allen. Watching a standup work out his personal struggles interspersed with scenes of his personal life will look familiar to fans of *Louie*. The relationship with Abby, at turns joyful and neurotic, also has a natural precedent in *Annie Hall*; the scene with the real-life Dr. Dement providing sleeping advice is especially Woody-like.

There are plenty of laughs and plenty of truth in *Sleepwalk.* It's plainly autobiographical, and the choice to rename the lead character and some of the minor characters is interesting. It will puzzle some who have followed these stories through different stages, but it's smart from a narrative standpoint. It allows Birbiglia a bit more room to shape events and change characters to heighten the drama. It's the choice of a filmmaker. It had better be. *My Girlfriend's Boyfriend* is next.

Sleepwalk With Me opens today in New York and around the country next week.

August 28, 2012

Robert Kelly
Robert Kelly Live (Reissue)
Stand Up! Records

By Elise Czajkowski

It's very difficult for observational comedy to hold up over time. Even solid material can age quickly as once-novel ideas become over-observed, and trends and references change with the wind. So Stand Up! Records's decision to reissue Robert Kelly's 2003 album, *Robert Kelly Live*, is an interesting one.

Kelly's reputation has undoubtedly grown in the intervening years. He toured the country with Dane Cook and was featured on Cook's 2006 HBO tour documentary, *Tourgasm.* In 2008, he released his second album, *Just the Tip.* More recently, he played Louis C.K.'s brother on the first season of *Louie,* and has been cast alongside fellow Comedy Cellar regular Godfrey in FX fall pilot *Bronx Warrants.*

On the other hand, a lot can change in nine years. It's hard to say whether this material was fresh when it was first released, but now it feels decidedly stale.

Kelly's stand up covers the well-trod ground of sex and scatological humor, mixed with some less-than-Earth-shattering remarks about New York's smells and raking leaves. It is, in some ways, the epitome of "Hey, I relate to that!" humor. That's not to say there is anything wrong with the subject matter, per se—all premises have the potential for new, fertile material. But Kelly fails to expand on his ideas in any meaningful way, and his set is mostly a list of shallow observations.

This means that he hits on a lot of topics, each for a very short period of time. It's difficult to determine whether it's a case of ruthless editing or if Kelly has some moral opposition to transitions, but the way he switches between subjects is dizzying. Occasionally the lack of segues feels a bit glib, like his abrupt shift from discussing the Taliban to his afternoon in a tanning salon, but mostly it's just confusing and kills any potential momentum.

The other problem with listening to a nearly decade-old album is that our social norms have undeniably evolved. Though it would be ridiculous to insinuate that homophobia is absent from comedy clubs these days, Kelly's tendency to describe things as "a little faggy" feels moored in a different era. His material about women is hardly more progressive, although it appears to have been antiquated even when it was recorded. When he learns that a male audience member doesn't play video games, he's dismissed immediately as "gay"; when a woman pipes up that she does, his retort is, "Okay, you fucking lesbian. Relax."

Overall, his thoughts on the fairer sex are less than complimentary, and with a track entitled "Women Are Evil," his intentions are not hidden. Despite that title, he doesn't come across as an overtly sexist person. The real problem is that his topics, such as women's unreasonableness or their lack of beauty upkeep once in a relationship, have been so thoroughly mined by everything from sitcoms to beer commercials that they lack any punch.

Similarly, his propensity for falling into ethnic intonations habitually walks the line of good taste. His annoyance at being mistaken for Mexican while visiting Los

Angeles or his take on the relative sexiness of accents is clearly based on his own experiences—he's not trying to win points through racial stereotyping. But he fails to add any substantial ideas to the discussion, making the need for comically exaggerated accents questionable.

It's not that Kelly seems like a bad guy. If anything, his tough-guy attitude feels like a false persona, and his attempts at righteous indignation ring hollow. His excessive use of profanities starts to feel like a crutch, an attempt to add heft to some very thin premises. It's when he flubs a line and mutters, "I'm such a douchebag," with an endearing giggle that a genuinely relatable side of his personality emerges.

There are a few good laughs. A bit about a blooper reel from Osama bin Laden's videos works well. And when he mentions how he's still afraid of the dark, and that he worries about monsters in the woods, he hints at a whole world of potentially interesting material in that more vulnerable arena.

The album's fairly generic title is unfortunately indicative of his voice and of the material, which lacks cohesion or overarching themes. (An attempt at a running joke about a "piss the pants monster" doesn't work or build to anything interesting.) At the same time, Kelly doesn't quite manage to establish a unique enough personality to encourage the audience to get on board with his particular point of view. (Fortunately he would go on to correct this imbalance on the more introspective and far superior *Just the Tip*.) It seems, then, that the decision to re-release *Robert Kelly Live* now must be solely related to Kelly's increased prominence, as the material itself is nowhere near memorable enough to deserve another rotation.

September 3, 2012

Brent Weinbach
Mostly Live
ASpecialThing Records

By Dyan Flores

Brent Weinbach is weird. Gloriously weird. Too many "weird" comedians rely on being strange as a distraction so the audience won't pay attention to whether or not their material is any good, but Weinbach's weirdness is genuine. It's magnetic. It's the main event, not the distraction. You're not sure what kind of brain comes up with material like his, but you're thankful for it and you'll give its owner your undivided attention.

Weinbach's third release, *Mostly Live*, features all-new material recorded mostly live (just like the title says!) at UCB LA,with some studio bits interspersed. Rather than your typical comedy album of traditional jokes or bits, the tracks vary from impressions to elaborately set-up stories to audience participation. It jumps from highbrow to lowbrow, from obscure to routine, from squeaky clean to raunchy, all in the blink of an eye. And as previously mentioned, it's weird, it's very funny, and parts of it border on genius.

Mostly Live opens with what one can only assume is a spot-on impression of a cunnilingus-loving YouTube pervert. (I personally don't have basis for comparison, but it seemed accurate.) Mind you, this impression is delivered with absolutely no preface, but it still works. That's one of the most impressive things about Weinbach's material. He's such a gifted comedian that audiences are willing to go to bizarre, uncomfortable places with him without justification. Sometimes he'll offer an explanation or some background information, but he sells his material so skillfully that it's not even necessary.

More often than not Weinbach mines the bizarre for material, but when he does turn to the mundane he examines it through a completely new filter. His Netflix joke starts off as a seemingly innocuous half-joke about Netflix for kids, but as he continues he reveals that he's actually proposing a service that mails out children in place of DVDs. A later joke about strip clubs turns into an uncomfortably funny audience-participation bit about the inherently perverse intent of friendly strip-club outings. While some comedians muse about the ordinary and seem to take the words right out of your mouth, Brent Weinbach warps the ordinary so much that you're not necessarily sure you know what it is anymore. He has a knack for making the pedestrian subversive.

One of the risks Weinbach takes that pays off in spades is his willingness to cover highbrow material. Though his topical comedy and raunchier jokes are well executed, some of the most rewarding jokes are his loftier ones. On an album where he impersonates a gay train and sings a song about taking pictures of his fecal matter, it might surprise some that jokes about Tuvan throat singing are right there alongside them. Perhaps the crowing glory of the album is "Latin," where Weinbach posits that someone who has forgotten the words to their Latin hymn (And who hasn't found themselves in such a situation?) could simply read the ingredients from a bag of Doritos (Because of course you have those handy in church.) Rather than shy away from such a premise he takes a leap of faith and hopes that the audience will rise to the occasion, which they can't help but do.

It helps that Brent Weinbach is incredibly clever, but it certainly doesn't hurt that he has an extremely unique voice—his actual voice, not his artistic voice, although that is also very original. Brent Weinbach's regular speaking voice sounds a little like Kermit the Frog, but despite his distinctive timbre, he has an uncanny knack at assuming different characters. When you're listening to his album it's easy to forget that it's even the same person the whole time. From an enthusiastic reggae performer to a mousy telemarketer, these eerily accurate impersonations come out of left field to impress and delight. When the Vietnamese-jazz-vocalist-who-works-as-a-waiter-during-the-daytime assumes the mic it takes only a few seconds to overcome the "What the hell?!" factor and savor this bit of nonsensical ingenuity. Weinbach has the kind of voice you'd listen to read the phone book, and in a hidden track, you get close to that when he recites the Russian alphabet.

For those who listen to *Mostly Live* or who get a chance to catch Brent Weinbach perform, it is imperative that they take their friends by the shoulders, look them squarely in the eye and implore them to become familiar with Weinbach's comedy. Because you really can't repeat one of his jokes without a lot of explanation and attempts at mimicry, and even then you're not going to get the inimitable delivery that makes his comedy so satisfying. He is a one-of-a-kind performer who must be experienced firsthand, and the more people who can understand that and share in the delight of Weinbach's weird ways, the better.

September 4, 2012

The Eugene Mirman Comedy Festival
The Bell House and Union Hall
September 13-16, 2012

By Elise Czajkowski

The Eugene Mirman Comedy Festival may have begun life as an off-hand joke, but over the last five years it has become a legitimately respected festival, this year pulling in superstars Sarah Silverman and Jim Gaffigan alongside international acts Daniel Kitson and David O'Doherty, plus local legends like Todd Barry and Tom Shillue. Despite the increasing prominence of the festival, Mirman's offbeat sensibility remained, from the program, which featured bios for all the performers written by Mirman himself, to the titles of such shows as "Comedians Two to Five Years Away From Their Own TV Shows."

"We did it!" Mirman began the first night's show, the appropriately titled "We Appreciate Ourselves: The Five Year Anniversary Celebration of the Eugene Mirman Comedy Festival." "We put on a bunch of shows…in a place convenient to me!" The eponymous founder was ubiquitous at the festival, appearing at six of the eight shows, and could be found every night taking pictures with fans and singing karaoke at the after-parties.

The after-parties themselves have become a legendary part of the festival. This year's included a slam poet at whom audience members could throw water balloons, a VIP Herring room with a selection of pickled and dried fish (some of which were actually eaten), a strobe-lit, booze-filled party bus and a full pig roasting outside The Bell House. The comedians tended to stick around as well, giving the entire event a casual atmosphere that can be lost at other, bigger festivals.

Despite—or perhaps because of—his ever-presence, Mirman happily shared the spotlight. Friday's main show was the science/comedy podcast *StarTalk*, hosted by Hayden Planetarium director and nerd favorite Neil deGrasse Tyson. The show, which stretched past the two-and-a-half-hour mark, was unlike anything seen at more mainstream comedy festivals, with extensive discussions about the possibilities of life on Mars and the future of American space travel.

It's shows like this where Mirman gets to have his cake and eat it, too. Since tickets to each show were sold individually, with no all-festival passes, the crowd for "*StarTalk* Live!" was filled with the show's devout fans, who were more than happy for in-depth science chat, even if it meant a few minutes without a joke. But the inclusion of Mirman, Silverman and Gaffigan on the panel made it funny enough for comedy fans to appreciate the show as well.

As all of the shows were held at 21-plus venues The Bell House and Union Hall, Saturday afternoon included a special all-ages show. The always-delightful Tom Shillue hosted, making it a cheery, casual and occasionally interactive show. "Uh Oh: Dangerous, Inappropriate Comedy for Teenagers—A Comedy Show For Sexually Active Teens* Or Families That Don't Feel Too Weird If Adult Subject Matter Is Discussed (*Teens Don't Actually Have To Be Sexually Active. In Fact, It's Better If You Wait 'Til Sophomore Year of College)" lived up to its extensive title. Acts like Ben Kronberg and Jacqueline Novak didn't shy away from their bawdier material, despite the presence of preteens in the crowd.

Saturday's headliner, Elna Baker and Kevin Townley's "The Variety Show," had a lot to live up to—last year's legendary "Drunk Show" featured Ira Glass and Leo Allen arm wrestling on the floor, and Glass ultimately blacking out. The theme this time around was the far more sedate "Speech and Debate," and featured improvised speeches and presentations on such topics as solitude and Tom's of Maine. Structured like a high-school debate competition, the pace of the show wavered at times. But the uniqueness of the format allowed brilliant minds like Mirman's and Barry's to show off their comic chops in new ways.

The highlight of the festival was Sunday night's headliner "Invite Them Up," a revival of the show once co-produced by Mirman and host Bobby Tisdale. The night featured drop-ins from John Oliver and Demetri Martin, as well as the festival's only on-stage nudity, in a fantastically surreal musical bit from H. Jon Benjamin and Larry Murphy. But the undeniable star of the night was English storyteller and acknowledged genius Daniel Kitson. Despite his assertion that he was put on last because of his inability to stay within a time limit, Kitson is truly an impossible act to follow, if only for his tendency to destroy everything on stage for his finale.

And so the festival ended with Kitson knocking over two microphone stands, pouring water into a little puddle on the stage, and then walking off silently as the crowd cheered. Those moments, rare gems of weirdness and hilarity, are the lifeblood of Mirman's endeavor. As long as it can manage to maintain that sense of unpredictability and nerdy enthusiasm, it will remain one of the world's most fun comedy festivals.

September 17, 2012

Weird Al: The Book
Nathan Rabin with Al Yankovic
Abrams Image

By Danny Gallagher

It's hard to imagine the career of a comedy musician lasting more than a few chart-toppers since it has to exist in the vacuum of the recording industry, a business so humorless that it sees nothing wrong with filing billion-dollar lawsuits against grandmothers for downloading a couple of songs while practicing creative accounting against the very artists who crafted them. It's even harder to imagine that industry would let an artist like "Weird Al" Yankovic carry on in the business after writing a "We Are the World"-esque ballad in 2006 called "Don't Download This Song." In fact, it's unfathomable to imagine he would be able to physically walk after releasing it for free on the Internet.

Somehow Yankovic has not only kept his throne as the premiere musical comedian for almost three decades. He's also lost it and fought back to regain it by reinventing what he does, somehow making it seem like he's done it the same way throughout his entire career.

The Onion A.V. Club's Nathan Rabin chronicles the rises and falls in *Weird Al: The Book*, the first definitive literary attempt to chronicle Yankovic's musical life from an accordion-playing teen to an accordion-playing pop-culture phenomenon. Yankovic wisely allows Rabin to take the reins for the bulk of the writing, providing an objective view of his career and parts of his personal life.

Rabin's style makes for an entertaining read that meshes perfectly with Yankovic's trademark sense of surreal and downright silly humor, whether it's his description of a hard-playing accordionist who looks like "the Michelin man in the midst of an asthma attack," the sudden halting of his James Blunt parody by industry suits or Eminem's refusal to let Yankovic do a "Lose Yourself" parody because "Eminem could handle anything, apparently, besides gentle mockery."

Serving more as a coffee-table book than official chronicle of the comedian's work, it's also filled with pictures and fan artwork compiled by drummer Jon "Bermuda" Schwartz, the official historian of Yankovic's career. Yankovic jumps in by offering witty, personalized captions as well as some choice jokes from his Twitter feed. These might just feel like layout filler, but they showcase his often-underrated ability to satirize and skewer beyond the bounds of popular music in ways that are actually funnier, which is harder to do than it looks. (He's got a killer Rupert Murdoch joke that could easily get big laughs on *The Colbert Report*.)

The limited space also means that Rabin has to move rather quickly, to the point where some diehard fans might find themselves asking why the book skips certain videos. Fortunately he knows where to mine for the choicest material and can deconstruct songs like "Frank's 2000-Inch TV" and "Smells Like Nirvana" as if they are as deep and philosophical as Neil Young's preachiest performance. He also knows that some songs like "The Night Santa Went Crazy" and "Party at the Leper Colony" were designed to do one thing: get intentional laughter out of its listeners. That accomplishment alone makes Yankovic a maverick in the

151

unintentional ridiculousness of the recording industry.

October 3, 2012

Tig Notaro
Live
Secretly Canadian

By Nick A. Zaino III

"Hello. Good evening, hello. I have cancer, how are you?"

That's how Tig Notaro opened her August 3 set at Largo shortly after being introduced by Ed Helms. People in the crowd are heard laughing nervously on *Live* (as in "continue to live," according to the album's PR), released Friday on Louis C.K.'s site as one 30-minute track. Is this some sort of performance stunt? Often comics will dig holes to see if they can climb out of them. That's not what's happening. "Just diagnosed with cancer," she finally says. "Oh, God." She pauses to take a few deep breaths, and it's clear this is no clever misdirection. This is a human being staring up at something bigger than herself, readying to take a big swing at it.

What follows is remarkable, not just as comedy, but on a human level. It's funny, raw and life-affirming. "It's weird because with humor, the equation is tragedy plus time equals comedy," observes Notaro, only a few days into her diagnosis of breast cancer at the time of the recording. "I am just at 'tragedy' right now. That's just where I am at the equation." Notaro allows her audience to watch her processing this information, in doing so granting both them and herself permission to laugh at it.

"They're like, 'Oh, we found a lump.'" she recalls of her mammogram. "I was like, 'Oh, no; that's my boob.'" They

153

find a lump on the other side. "I was like, 'Yeah, I've got one over there, too. Those are my boobs.'" She describes the pain she felt from the biopsy, eliciting moans of sympathy from an audience member. Notaro addresses it immediately, asking, "Who's taking this really bad?" She tells them it's going to be okay and receives applause, then catches herself. "I'm just saying you're going to be okay. I don't know what's going on with me."

It's clear even on the recording that the air has gone out of the room, and that performer and audience are experiencing this completely in the moment. Notaro regresses four months to another near-death experience in the hospital, tragic news about her mother and a break up prior to her diagnosis. It's okay, she jokes, because God never gives you more than you can handle. She pictures God saying, "You know what, I think she can take a little more," while his angels tell him he's out of his mind.

Notaro says she just wants to be able to have a normal conversation, to have her friends know it's okay to describe their bad day without feeling guilty, or to be able to set up a dating profile...with the caveat "Serious inquiries only." At one point she stops to marvel at what she's accomplished in her career, and how no one can see what's waiting for them. Sensing she's getting too introspective, she asks, "What if I just transitioned right now into silly, just jokes right now?" The audience won't let her. "This is fucking amazing," says one. Hard to top that description. This is why human beings developed comedy in the first place.

October 8, 2012

Ryan Singer
Comedy Wonder Town
Stand Up! Records

By John Wenzel

Zany cover art and title aside, Ryan Singer's *Comedy Wonder Town* doesn't contain a great deal of laughs or insight until about halfway through, when Singer dials down the dick jokes and asks the audience to go a bit deeper.

The opening tracks aren't terrible, mind you. They just happen to sound like a road dog's late-night material from two decades ago—pleasant but overdone, and lacking an interesting point of view. "I could never date a woman who has murdered somebody before, because I know I would never, ever again win another fight or argument for the rest of my life," Singer says on "Death Row Love." "No matter how committed I am to my side of the cause, clearly she's willing to see this shit all the way to the end. She's got a short fuse and follow-through, bro. You betta watch yo *ass.*"

Singer's buddy-buddy tone and avalanche of "bro"s and "dude"s feel eager-to-please, especially since the bits are so rapidly delivered and self-contained that they verge on catchphrases. But this is a comedy album, after all, and packing 24 tracks into 52 minutes isn't necessarily a bad thing.

Then Singer invokes the title of the album—which was recorded, like his 2010 debut *How to Get High Without Drugs*, at Go Bananas in Cincinnati—and things get interesting. "Here's a rule about Comedy Wonder Town," he says, his mild Appalachian drawl barely containing a certain L.A. unctuousness, like a Blue Collar Comedy version of *Parks and Recreation* character Jean-Ralphio. "You have to keep an open heart and an open mind. Some of this shit might get a little weird. But I'm always going to throw you a life preserver in the shape of a dick joke. So if you feel yourself drowning in that weirdness, grab onto that dick, citizen, and come back to the boat."

At 5:10, "Hands That Built Human History" is the second-longest track on an album that flies by like a Guided by Voices LP—patched together, loose and short on the usual filler. (Is it a coincidence that, like GBV leader Robert Pollard, Singer is also a former schoolteacher from Dayton, Ohio?) But afterwards, Singer sounds more exploratory and fearless. Perhaps it's a function of joke-sequencing, or his rhythmic energy, but it propels the album into new and far more interesting territory.

We get to hear a delicate tension between style and material, between a fast-talking, at times overly-affected voice and clever observational punchlines. Singer offers a bit of character work on "Two Rooms Available," "Why Won't She Love Me" and "Monster Hunter," briefly flashing his vocal range. And when he gets to "Babies Having Babies" and "Proper Neanderthal Family," the awkward silence from the audience feels like a validation of his joyously bizarre ideas. (Think in-utero intercourse and emo cavemen.)

He smartly weighs the difference between necessity and luxury with "Put Me on the List" and gets stoner-ontological with "I Know Zero" and "Letters and Numbers," which in their own ways do justice to the great Mitch Hedberg. "Astronauts are nerds with *huge nuts*," he says on

"People in Space," and you almost want to leap up and cheer in agreement. You just wish he would have gotten there sooner.

October 16, 2012

Zizzle Zazzles: An Evening with Rory Scovel
UCB Chelsea
November 8, 2012

By Elise Czajkowski

With an alt favorite like Rory Scovel, there's always the worry that the hype will overwhelm the material. After witnessing him do a concurrent set with Jon Dore on *Conan* or pitching open-mic bits while climbing onstage scaffolding, there's a real possibility that seeing a conventional headlining performance could disappoint.

Luckily for the New York Comedy Festival audience at *Zizzle Zazzles*, it was everything fans could want from a Scovel show. For one thing, the Southern-inflected German accent that he maintained throughout—unacknowledged until the final minute—imbued every line with a slightly surreal humor. If nothing else, it's an impressive feat to get through an entire hour without pronouncing a single "th" sound. (Try saying the word "atheist" without it.)

The secret to Scovel's success may be that his prepared material is clever enough to stand on its own. His proposition that Christopher Columbus was "the greatest real-estate agent ever" and the storylines he creates when washing dishes while high are well-developed and hilarious bits. The surrounding silliness of ad-libs and characters only work because he builds on such strong premises, a principle lost on many who attempt "wackiness" without a solid base.

But it's definitely in his extemporizing that Scovel cements his status as one of the funniest comics working today. A physical chunk that began when he accidentally stepped on the mic cord and ended with him continuing his set while Tebowing had a taste of the you-had-to-be-there magic of great improv shows. And part of the joy of his clearly off-the-cuff miming of a One Percenter smoking a cigarette was his own amusement in the idea, his face going red as he cracked up.

Ordinarily, a standup laughing at his own jokes wears thin, because the comic is normally attempting to overcompensate for the audience's lack of amusement. But watching Scovel entertain himself is more like seeing an actor break during a *SNL* sketch—a sign that he's experiencing it all with the audience and is just as amazed by how funny it all is.

With a headliner like Scovel, opener Mike Kaiser was bound to be overlooked. "Who am I?" he began his set, a question the crowd clearly wondered about this unannounced opener. Nonetheless, Kasier's attempt to distinguish himself from the "15,000 young, slender, bearded white comics in New York City" was promising, with a particularly great joke involving William Faulkner and salamanders, and a string of "It's so cold out…" gags that suggest he has a bright future in writing late-night monologue jokes.

"Me and 75 percent of the audience are really into this show," Scovel said halfway through his set. "Twenty-five percent aren't sure it's started yet." It's impossible to say what the next incarnation will be like, or the one after that. Presumably each performance of *Zizzle Zazzles* will bring its own unpredictable weirdness. It's always worth going to find out.

November 8, 2012

Brian Regan
The Beacon Theatre
November 9, 2012

By Daniel Berkowitz

A comedian walks onto the stage of a nearly packed venue
that seats almost 3000 people. Each has bought their tickets
for the New York Comedy Festival event in advance, and
paid a pretty penny to do so. The comedian tells his jokes for
exactly one hour. He never once loses the crowd; he
consistently has the audience roaring like hyenas; he allows
their money to be well spent.

How does one criticize a comedian like this?

When Brian Regan took the stage at the Beacon
Theatre, every person in the crowd knew what they were
going to witness. They were going to hear Regan wax faux-
stupid. They were going to see him make hilariously bizarre
faces. They were going to hear him relate his awkward social
experiences. They were going to see his patented arms-wide-
out pacing.

He'd squint his eyes. He'd yell into the microphone.
He'd make 'em laugh. Everyone knew this, and they received
exactly what they were looking for.

Yet Regan doesn't pander. If he did, his comedy
would be decidedly more stale and lame. The sticking point
with his act, however, is how safe it is. Regan, in effect, never
takes a risk. Some might say he doesn't have to: he's too
funny as is, and his voice is so distinct that to venture into
rough seas might constitute a betrayal of his true personality.
If Regan dared to just once utter a four-letter word or allude

to a female body part, he wouldn't be himself, and his comedy would therefore be disingenuous.

To believe something along these lines, though, is a challenge to any comedian who considers him- or herself— or, whom we consider—an artist. To be an artist as a comedian is to ultimately grow as a person. The definition lies in the channeling of an inner vision, or rather, in the struggle to channel it. The art is in the process.

Regan, by comparison, does not seem to struggle with anything. He has one foot in that vaunted Jay Leno camp of safe and clean comedy—that insular cocoon where pushing boundaries and challenging others means less ears and eyes.

It's not a calculated move, but it is a choice. And that choice is to not alienate anyone. By limiting how much of his true self he puts into his act, Regan is able to selectively mask his flaws. The bold and the brave comedians, on the other hand, do not mask their flaws; they embrace them. They talk about them. They work through them.

None of this is to say that Regan is not a gifted performer. Nor is it to say the several thousand people who came to the Beacon were given a phony or half-assed performance. Far from it. Regan put on a damn fine show. Hell, if one watched his entire 60-minute set and 10-minute encore and disagreed, then that person would simply be lying. The truth is, Regan killed. Regan slayed those 3000 sets of ears and eyes. His fans left happy, equilibrium was maintained, and all was right in the safe cocoon of clean comedy. But was it art?

November 10, 2012

Acknowledgements

Contributors Josh Bell, Daniel Berkowitz, Patrick Bromley, Elise Czajkowski, Dyan Flores, Danny Gallagher, Steve Heisler, Austin Ray, Michael Tedder, John Wenzel, and Nick Zaino must first and foremost be commended for their skill, enthusiasm, and formidable expertise in all comedic matters. Daniel Berkowitz in particular has been an indispensable asset in the position of editorial assistant, his tireless work ethic remaining an integral component of both the ongoing *Spit Take* web presence as well as the formatting of this compilation.

The Spit Take would not exist without the progressive vision and community spirit at the heart of the Brown Paper Tickets organization. A large debt of gratitude is due to Steve Butcher, with additional appreciation owed for the tireless efforts of William Jordan, Mike Sennett, Sten Iverson, Barb Morgen, AJ Andrews, Beth Lambert, Joel Kalonji, Jimmy Berg, Rachel Wong, and Karen Chappell, plus comrades in arts Graeme Thomas, Randy "Bob Noxious" Hughes, Bill Geoghegan, Sabrina Roach, Tamara Clammer, and Kelly Allen.

Special thanks to Lauren Wood for her passion, TJ Young for his visual wizardry, and Chris Elles and Matt Kleinschmidt for their business acumen and open-door policy. Last but certainly not least, the manifold talents of Todd Jackson have for several years transformed the comedy industry for the better. Not only does Todd do it all, he does it for all the right reasons.

More than anything, the opportunity to enjoy, discuss, and write about comedy wholly depends upon legions of original, tenacious, beautifully flawed performers slugging it out night after night. From open micers to late legends, you make our world a more interesting, joyous, and enlightened place to inhabit…and provide some of us with the inspiration to even bother dealing with any of it in the first place.